Promises
for Women from
GOD'S WORD

BakerBooks

a division of Baker Publishing Group
Grand Rapids, Michigan

GOD'S WORD® is copyright 1995 by God's Word to the Nations.
Used by permission of Baker Publishing Group. All rights reserved.

Published by Baker Books
a division of Baker Publishing Group
P.O. Box 6287, Grand Rapids, MI 49516-6287
www.bakerbooks.com

ISBN 978-0-8010-1465-9

ISBN 978-0-8010-1396-6 (pbk.)

Printed in the United States of America

11 12 13 14 15 16 17   7 6 5 4 3 2

Contents

God Promises to Meet Women's Need for . . .

God Promises to Help Women Grow in . . .

God Promises to Help Grow Women of . . .

God Promises That He Will Be Faithful to . . .

God Promises to Strengthen Women in Their . . .

God Keeps His Promises through . . .

Women Can Believe God's Promises Because of His . . .

Faithfulness

Keep in mind that the Lord your God is the only God. He is a faithful God, who keeps his promise and is merciful to thousands of generations of those who love him and obey his commands.

Deuteronomy 7:9

I will sing forever about the evidence of your mercy,
    O Lord.
I will tell about your faithfulness to every
    generation.
I said, "Your mercy will last forever.
    Your faithfulness stands firm in the heavens."

Psalm 89:1–2

The Lord is good.
    His mercy endures forever.
    His faithfulness endures throughout every
        generation.

Psalm 100:5

The Lord is fair in all his ways
    and faithful in everything he does.

Psalm 145:17

The reason I can still find hope is that I keep this one
        thing in mind:
    the LORD's mercy.
        We were not completely wiped out.
        His compassion is never limited.
            It is new every morning.
            His faithfulness is great.

                                    Lamentations 3:21–23

God faithfully keeps his promises. He called you to be
partners with his Son Jesus Christ our Lord.

                                    1 Corinthians 1:9

There isn't any temptation that you have experienced
which is unusual for humans. God, who faithfully keeps
his promises, will not allow you to be tempted beyond
your power to resist. But when you are tempted, he will
also give you the ability to endure the temptation as your
way of escape.

                                    1 Corinthians 10:13

But the Lord is faithful and will strengthen you and
protect you against the evil one.

                                    2 Thessalonians 3:3

God is faithful and reliable. If we confess our sins, he
forgives them and cleanses us from everything we've done
wrong.

                                    1 John 1:9

Goodness

Do not remember the sins of my youth or my rebellious ways.
   Remember me, O Lord, in keeping with your mercy
      and your goodness.
The Lord is good and decent.
   That is why he teaches sinners the way they should live.

Psalm 25:7–8

Taste and see that the Lord is good.
   Blessed is the person who takes refuge in him.

Psalm 34:8

The Lord is good.
   His mercy endures forever.
   His faithfulness endures throughout every generation.

Psalm 100:5

Give thanks to the Lord because he is good,
   because his mercy endures forever.

Psalm 136:1

The LORD is good to those who wait for him,
to anyone who seeks help from him.

Lamentations 3:25

The LORD is good.
He is a fortress in the day of trouble.
He knows those who seek shelter in him.

Nahum 1:7

Even though you're evil, you know how to give good
gifts to your children. So how much more will your Father
in heaven give good things to those who ask him?

Matthew 7:11

Every good present and every perfect gift comes from
above, from the Father who made the sun, moon, and stars.
The Father doesn't change like the shifting shadows pro-
duced by the sun and the moon.

James 1:17

Kingdom

Blessed are those who recognize they are spiritually
helpless.
The kingdom of heaven belongs to them.

Matthew 5:3

But first, be concerned about his kingdom and what has
his approval. Then all these things will be provided for you.

Matthew 6:33

Whoever becomes like this little child is the greatest in
the kingdom of heaven.

Matthew 18:4

God has rescued us from the power of darkness and has
brought us into the kingdom of his Son, whom he loves.

Colossians 1:13

You know very well that we treated each of you the
way a father treats his children. We comforted you and
encouraged you. Yet, we insisted that you should live in a
way that proves you belong to the God who calls you into
his kingdom and glory.

1 Thessalonians 2:11–12

Therefore, we must be thankful that we have a kingdom that cannot be shaken. Because we are thankful, we must serve God with fear and awe in a way that pleases him.

Hebrews 12:28

Love

The LORD appeared to me in a faraway place and
      said,
"I love you with an everlasting love.
   So I will continue to show you my kindness."

                                    Jeremiah 31:3

God loved the world this way: He gave his only Son
so that everyone who believes in him will not die but will
have eternal life.

                                       John 3:16

I am in them, and you are in me. So they are completely
united. In this way the world knows that you have sent me
and that you have loved them in the same way you have
loved me.

                                      John 17:23

I am convinced that nothing can ever separate us from
God's love which Christ Jesus our Lord shows us. We can't
be separated by death or life, by angels or rulers, by anything in the present or anything in the future, by forces
or powers in the world above or in the world below, or by
anything else in creation.

                                  Romans 8:38–39

Clearly, Christ's love guides us. We are convinced of the fact that one man has died for all people. Therefore, all people have died. He died for all people so that those who live should no longer live for themselves but for the man who died and was brought back to life for them.

2 Corinthians 5:14–15

But God is rich in mercy because of his great love for us. We were dead because of our failures, but he made us alive together with Christ. (It is God's kindness that saved you.)

Ephesians 2:4–5

This way, with all of God's people you will be able to understand how wide, long, high, and deep his love is. You will know Christ's love, which goes far beyond any knowledge. I am praying this so that you may be completely filled with God.

Ephesians 3:18–19

Consider this: The Father has given us his love. He loves us so much that we are actually called God's dear children. And that's what we are. For this reason the world doesn't recognize us, and it didn't recognize him either.

1 John 3:1

We have known and believed that God loves us. God is love. Those who live in God's love live in God, and God lives in them.

God's love has reached its goal in us. So we look ahead with confidence to the day of judgment. While we are in this world, we are exactly like him with regard to love.

1 John 4:16–17

Mercy

Mercy and truth have met.
Righteousness and peace have kissed.
Truth sprouts from the ground,
    and righteousness looks down from heaven.
The LORD will certainly give us what is good,
    and our land will produce crops.
Righteousness will go ahead of him
    and make a path for his steps.

Psalm 85:10–13

The LORD is compassionate, merciful, patient,
    and always ready to forgive.

Psalm 103:8

But from everlasting to everlasting,
    the LORD's mercy is on those who fear him.
    His righteousness belongs
        to their children and grandchildren,
        to those who are faithful to his promise.

Psalm 103:17–18

The LORD is merciful, compassionate, patient,
    and always ready to forgive.

Psalm 145:8

Let wicked people abandon their ways.
Let evil people abandon their thoughts.
Let them return to the LORD,
    and he will show compassion to them.
Let them return to our God,
    because he will freely forgive them.

Isaiah 55:7

Even if he makes us suffer,
    he will have compassion
        in keeping with the richness of his mercy.

Lamentations 3:32

Tear your hearts, not your clothes.
    Return to the LORD your God.
        He is merciful and compassionate,
            patient, and always ready to forgive
                and to change his plans about disaster.

Joel 2:13

Who is a God like you?
    You forgive sin
        and overlook the rebellion of your faithful
            people.
    You will not be angry forever,
        because you would rather show mercy.
    You will again have compassion on us.
    You will overcome our wrongdoing.
    You will throw all our sins into the deep sea.

Micah 7:18–19

Blessed are those who show mercy.
They will be treated mercifully.

Matthew 5:7

A new day will dawn on us from above
because our God is loving and merciful.

Luke 1:78

Therefore, God's choice does not depend on a person's desire or effort, but on God's mercy.

Romans 9:16

So we can go confidently to the throne of God's kindness to receive mercy and find kindness, which will help us at the right time.

Hebrews 4:16

Praise the God and Father of our Lord Jesus Christ! God has given us a new birth because of his great mercy. We have been born into a new life that has a confidence which is alive because Jesus Christ has come back to life.

1 Peter 1:3

Power

The victory for righteous people comes from the
   LORD.
   He is their fortress in times of trouble.
The LORD helps them and rescues them.
He rescues them from wicked people.
He saves them because they have taken refuge in
   him.

Psalm 37:39–40

My soul waits calmly for God alone.
   My salvation comes from him.
He alone is my rock and my savior—my stronghold.
   I cannot be severely shaken.

Psalm 62:1–2

As the mountains surround Jerusalem,
   so the LORD surrounds his people now and
      forever.

Psalm 125:2

The name of the LORD is a strong tower.
   A righteous person runs to it and is safe.

Proverbs 18:10

Look! God is my Savior.
I am confident and unafraid,
  because the Lord is my strength and my song.
  He is my Savior.

Isaiah 12:2

Finally, receive your power from the Lord and from his mighty strength. Put on all the armor that God supplies. In this way you can take a stand against the devil's strategies.

Ephesians 6:10–11

For this reason I suffer as I do. However, I'm not ashamed. I know whom I trust. I'm convinced that he is able to protect what he had entrusted to me until that day.

2 Timothy 1:12

Presence with His People

You make the path of life known to me.
Complete joy is in your presence.
Pleasures are by your side forever.

Psalm 16:11

The LORD is near to those whose hearts are humble.
He saves those whose spirits are crushed.

Psalm 34:18

Where can I go to get away from your Spirit?
Where can I run to get away from you?
If I go up to heaven, you are there.
If I make my bed in hell, you are there.
If I climb upward on the rays of the morning sun
or land on the most distant shore of the sea
where the sun sets
even there your hand would guide me
and your right hand would hold on to me.

Psalm 139:7–10

Where two or three have come together in my name, I
am there among them.

Matthew 18:20

I will not leave you all alone. I will come back to you. In a little while the world will no longer see me, but you will see me. You will live because I live. On that day you will know that I am in my Father and that you are in me and that I am in you.

John 14:18–20

Jesus answered him, "Those who love me will do what I say. My Father will love them, and we will go to them and make our home with them."

John 14:23

I am the vine. You are the branches. Those who live in me while I live in them will produce a lot of fruit. But you can't produce anything without me.

John 15:5

Come close to God, and he will come close to you.

James 4:8

This is how we will know that we belong to the truth and how we will be reassured in his presence. Whenever our conscience condemns us, we will be reassured that God is greater than our conscience and knows everything.

1 John 3:19–20

Purpose

The LORD's plan stands firm forever.
His thoughts stand firm in every generation.

Psalm 33:11

I will give you a new heart and put a new spirit in you.
I will remove your stubborn hearts and give you obedient
hearts. I will put my Spirit in you. I will enable you to live
by my laws, and you will obey my rules. Then you will
live in the land that I gave your ancestors. You will be my
people, and I will be your God.

Ezekiel 36:26–28

We know that all things work together for the good of
those who love God—those whom he has called according
to his plan.

Romans 8:28

Through the blood of his Son, we are set free from our
sins. God forgives our failures because of his overflowing
kindness. He poured out his kindness by giving us every
kind of wisdom and insight when he revealed the mystery
of his plan to us. He had decided to do this through Christ.

Ephesians 1:7–9

Then they sang a new song,
> "You deserve to take the scroll and open the seals
>> on it,
>> because you were slaughtered.
> You bought people with your blood to be God's
>> own.
>> They are from every tribe, language, people,
>>> and nation.
> You made them a kingdom and priests for our
>> God.
>> They will rule as kings on the earth."

Revelation 5:9–10

Son

He was the source of life, and that life was the light for humanity.

John 1:4

However, he gave the right to become God's children to everyone who believed in him. These people didn't become God's children in a physical way—from a human impulse or from a husband's desire to have a child. They were born from God.

John 1:12–13

God loved the world this way: He gave his only Son so that everyone who believes in him will not die but will have eternal life. God sent his Son into the world, not to condemn the world, but to save the world.

John 3:16–17

Jesus answered her, "Everyone who drinks this water will become thirsty again. But those who drink the water that I will give them will never become thirsty again. In fact, the water I will give them will become in them a spring that gushes up to eternal life."

John 4:13–14

Jesus said to her, "I am the one who brings people back to life, and I am life itself. Those who believe in me will live even if they die. Everyone who lives and believes in me will never die. Do you believe that?"

John 11:25–26

This is why God has given him an exceptional
    honor—
  the name honored above all other names—
    so that at the name of Jesus everyone in heaven,
      on earth,
    and in the world below will kneel
      and confess that Jesus Christ is Lord
        to the glory of God the Father.

Philippians 2:9–11

We, however, are citizens of heaven. We look forward to the Lord Jesus Christ coming from heaven as our Savior. Through his power to bring everything under his authority, he will change our humble bodies and make them like his glorified body.

Philippians 3:20–21

All of God lives in Christ's body, and God has made you complete in Christ. Christ is in charge of every ruler and authority.

Colossians 2:9–10

Because Christ offered himself to God, he is able to bring a new promise from God. Through his death he paid the price to set people free from the sins they committed under the first promise. He did this so that those who are called can be guaranteed an inheritance that will last forever.

Hebrews 9:15

Word

The teachings of the LORD are perfect.
  They renew the soul.
The testimony of the LORD is dependable.
  It makes gullible people wise.
The instructions of the LORD are correct.
  They make the heart rejoice.
The command of the LORD is radiant.
  It makes the eyes shine.

Psalm 19:7–8

O LORD, your word is established in heaven forever.

Psalm 119:89

Your word is a lamp for my feet
  and a light for my path.

Psalm 119:105

The earth and the heavens will disappear, but my words
will never disappear.

Mark 13:31

Every Scripture passage is inspired by God. All of them are useful for teaching, pointing out errors, correcting people, and training them for a life that has God's approval. They equip God's servants so that they are completely prepared to do good things.

2 Timothy 3:16–17

God's word is living and active. It is sharper than any two-edged sword and cuts as deep as the place where soul and spirit meet, the place where joints and marrow meet. God's word judges a person's thoughts and intentions.

Hebrews 4:12

God Promises to Be with
Women in Times of . . .

Adversity

He hides me in his shelter when there is trouble.
He keeps me hidden in his tent.
He sets me high on a rock.

Psalm 27:5

When I said, "My feet are slipping,"
    your mercy, O Lord, continued to hold me up.
When I worried about many things,
    your assuring words soothed my soul.

Psalm 94:18–19

But he told me: "My kindness is all you need. My power is strongest when you are weak." So I will brag even more about my weaknesses in order that Christ's power will live in me.

2 Corinthians 12:9

My brothers and sisters, be very happy when you are tested in different ways. You know that such testing of your faith produces endurance. Endure until your testing is over. Then you will be mature and complete, and you won't need anything.

James 1:2–4

Dear friends, don't be surprised by the fiery troubles that are coming in order to test you. Don't feel as though something strange is happening to you, but be happy as you share Christ's sufferings. Then you will also be full of joy when he appears again in his glory.

1 Peter 4:12–13

Those who suffer because that is God's will for them must entrust themselves to a faithful creator and continue to do what is good.

1 Peter 4:19

Challenge

I can't find him because he knows the road I take.
When he tests me,
    I'll come out as pure as gold.

Job 23:10

Turn your burdens over to the LORD,
    and he will take care of you.
        He will never let the righteous person stumble.

Psalm 55:22

With God we will display great strength.
    He will trample our enemies.

Psalm 60:12

It is better to depend on the LORD
    than to trust mortals.
It is better to depend on the LORD
    than to trust influential people.

Psalm 118:8–9

Don't you know?
  Haven't you heard?
The eternal God, the LORD, the Creator of the ends
    of the earth,
  doesn't grow tired or become weary.
    His understanding is beyond reach.
He gives strength to those who grow tired
  and increases the strength of those who are weak.
Even young people grow tired and become weary,
  and young men will stumble and fall.
Yet, the strength of those who wait with hope in the
    LORD
  will be renewed.
    They will soar on wings like eagles.
      They will run and won't become weary.
      They will walk and won't grow tired.

                              Isaiah 40:28–31

The Almighty LORD helps me.
  That is why I will not be ashamed.
    I have set my face like a flint.
      I know that I will not be put to shame.

                              Isaiah 50:7

You are extremely happy about these things, even though you have to suffer different kinds of trouble for a little while now. The purpose of these troubles is to test your faith as fire tests how genuine gold is. Your faith is more precious than gold, and by passing the test, it gives praise, glory, and honor to God. This will happen when Jesus Christ appears again.

                              1 Peter 1:6–7

Change

Even though I walk through the dark valley of
    death,
    because you are with me, I fear no harm.
        Your rod and your staff give me courage.

Psalm 23:4

A person's steps are directed by the Lord,
    and the Lord delights in his way.
When he falls, he will not be thrown down headfirst
    because the Lord holds on to his hand.

Psalm 37:23–24

A righteous person will always be remembered.
    He is not afraid of bad news.
    His heart remains secure, full of confidence in the
        Lord.
    His heart is steady, and he is not afraid.
        In the end he will look triumphantly at his
        enemies.

Psalm 112:6–8

The LORD guards you from every evil.
   He guards your life.
The LORD guards you as you come and go,
   now and forever.

Psalm 121:7–8

Conflict

The LORD will give power to his people.
The LORD will bless his people with peace.

Psalm 29:11

With his peace, he will rescue my soul
from the war waged against me,
because there are many soldiers fighting against
me.

Psalm 55:18

O LORD, blessed is the person
whom you discipline and instruct from your
teachings.
You give him peace and quiet from times of
trouble
while a pit is dug to trap wicked people.

Psalm 94:12–13

When a person's ways are pleasing to the LORD,
he makes even his enemies to be at peace with
him.

Proverbs 16:7

"The mountains may move, and the hills may shake,
but my kindness will never depart from you.
My promise of peace will never change,"
says the LORD, who has compassion on you.

Isaiah 54:10

All your children will be taught by the LORD,
and your children will have unlimited peace.

Isaiah 54:13

He will give light to those who live in the dark
and in death's shadow.
He will guide us into the way of peace.

Luke 1:79

Danger

The LORD is my light and my salvation.
  Who is there to fear?
The LORD is my life's fortress.
  Who is there to be afraid of?

Psalm 27:1

God is our refuge and strength,
  an ever-present help in times of trouble.
That is why we are not afraid
  even when the earth quakes
    or the mountains topple into the depths of the
      sea.
      Water roars and foams,
        and mountains shake at the surging waves.

Psalm 46:1–3

You do not need to fear
   terrors of the night,
   arrows that fly during the day,
   plagues that roam the dark,
   epidemics that strike at noon.
      They will not come near you,
         even though a thousand may fall dead beside
            you
            or ten thousand at your right side.

Psalm 91:5–7

Don't be afraid, because I am with you.
Don't be intimidated; I am your God.
   I will strengthen you.
   I will help you.
   I will support you with my victorious right hand.

Isaiah 41:10

No fear exists where his love is. Rather, perfect love gets rid of fear, because fear involves punishment. The person who lives in fear doesn't have perfect love.

1 John 4:18

Disappointment

They cried to you and were saved.
They trusted you and were never disappointed.

Psalm 22:5

His anger lasts only a moment.
His favor lasts a lifetime.
  Weeping may last for the night,
    but there is a song of joy in the morning.

Psalm 30:5

The Lord is near to those whose hearts are humble.
He saves those whose spirits are crushed.

Psalm 34:18

All goes well for the person who is generous and
        lends willingly.
    He earns an honest living.
        He will never fail.
        A righteous person will always be remembered.
            He is not afraid of bad news.
            His heart remains secure, full of confidence
                in the LORD.
            His heart is steady, and he is not afraid.
                In the end he will look triumphantly at his
                    enemies.

Psalm 112:5–8

In every way we're troubled, but we aren't crushed by
our troubles. We're frustrated, but we don't give up. We're
persecuted, but we're not abandoned. We're captured, but
we're not killed.

2 Corinthians 4:8–9

Doubt

Look! God is my Savior.
I am confident and unafraid,
    because the LORD is my strength and my song.
    He is my Savior.

Isaiah 12:2

With perfect peace you will protect those whose
        minds cannot be changed,
    because they trust you.
Trust the LORD always,
    because the LORD, the LORD alone, is an everlast-
        ing rock.

Isaiah 26:3–4

Jesus said to him, "As far as possibilities go, everything
is possible for the person who believes."
    The child's father cried out at once, "I believe! Help
my lack of faith."

Mark 9:23–24

Then the apostles said to the Lord, "Give us more faith."

The Lord said, "If you have faith the size of a mustard seed, you could say to this mulberry tree, 'Pull yourself up by the roots, and plant yourself in the sea!' and it would obey you."

Luke 17:5–6

He didn't doubt God's promise out of a lack of faith. Instead, giving honor to God for the promise, he became strong because of faith and was absolutely confident that God would do what he promised. That is why Abraham's faith was regarded as the basis of his approval by God.

Romans 4:20–22

Indeed, our lives are guided by faith, not by sight.

2 Corinthians 5:7

We must continue to hold firmly to our declaration of faith. The one who made the promise is faithful.

Hebrews 10:23

If any of you needs wisdom to know what you should do, you should ask God, and he will give it to you. God is generous to everyone and doesn't find fault with them. When you ask for something, don't have any doubts. A person who has doubts is like a wave that is blown by the wind and tossed by the sea.

James 1:5–6

Failure

The LORD is merciful, compassionate, patient,
and always ready to forgive.

Psalm 145:8

The Pharisees and their experts in Moses' Teachings
complained to Jesus' disciples. They asked, "Why do you
eat and drink with tax collectors and sinners?"

Jesus answered them, "Healthy people don't need a
doctor; those who are sick do. I've come to call sinners to
change the way they think and act, not to call people who
think they have God's approval."

Luke 5:30–31

Jesus, our Lord, was handed over to death because of
our failures and was brought back to life so that we could
receive God's approval.

Romans 4:25

Therefore, God's choice does not depend on a person's
desire or effort, but on God's mercy.

Romans 9:16

Through the blood of his Son, we are set free from our sins. God forgives our failures because of his overflowing kindness. He poured out his kindness by giving us every kind of wisdom and insight when he revealed the mystery of his plan to us. He had decided to do this through Christ.

Ephesians 1:7–9

You were once dead because of your failures and your uncircumcised corrupt nature. But God made you alive with Christ when he forgave all our failures.

Colossians 2:13

God saved us and called us to be holy, not because of what we had done, but because of his own plan and kindness. Before the world began, God planned that Christ Jesus would show us God's kindness.

2 Timothy 1:9

Fear and Anxiety

I always keep the LORD in front of me.
  When he is by my side, I cannot be moved.
    That is why my heart is glad and my soul
      rejoices.
    My body rests securely.

Psalm 16:8–9

Even though I walk through the dark valley of
  death,
  because you are with me, I fear no harm.
    Your rod and your staff give me courage.

Psalm 23:4

The LORD is my light and my salvation.
  Who is there to fear?
The LORD is my life's fortress.
  Who is there to be afraid of?

Psalm 27:1

I went to the LORD for help.
  He answered me and rescued me from all my
    fears.

Psalm 34:4

Even when I am afraid, I still trust you.

Psalm 56:3

You, O Lord, are my refuge!
You have made the Most High your home.
No harm will come to you.
No sickness will come near your house.
He will put his angels in charge of you
to protect you in all your ways.
They will carry you in their hands
so that you never hit your foot against a
rock.
You will step on lions and cobras.
You will trample young lions and snakes.

Psalm 91:9–13

When I worried about many things,
your assuring words soothed my soul.

Psalm 94:19

A person's anxiety will weigh him down,
but an encouraging word makes him joyful.

Proverbs 12:25

Don't be afraid, because I am with you.
Don't be intimidated; I am your God.
I will strengthen you.
I will help you.
I will support you with my victorious right hand.

Isaiah 41:10

I, the LORD your God, hold your right hand
   and say to you, "Don't be afraid; I will help you."

Isaiah 41:13

So I tell you to stop worrying about what you will eat, drink, or wear. Isn't life more than food and the body more than clothes?

Look at the birds. They don't plant, harvest, or gather the harvest into barns. Yet, your heavenly Father feeds them. Aren't you worth more than they?

Can any of you add a single hour to your life by worrying?

And why worry about clothes? Notice how the flowers grow in the field. They never work or spin yarn for clothes. But I say that not even Solomon in all his majesty was dressed like one of these flowers. That's the way God clothes the grass in the field. Today it's alive, and tomorrow it's thrown into an incinerator. So how much more will he clothe you people who have so little faith? . . .

So don't ever worry about tomorrow. After all, tomorrow will worry about itself. Each day has enough trouble of its own.

Matthew 6:25–30, 34

Don't be troubled. Believe in God, and believe in me.

John 14:1

Never worry about anything. But in every situation let God know what you need in prayers and requests while giving thanks. Then God's peace, which goes beyond anything we can imagine, will guard your thoughts and emotions through Christ Jesus.

Philippians 4:6–7

Turn all your anxiety over to God because he cares for you.

1 Peter 5:7

No fear exists where his love is. Rather, perfect love gets rid of fear, because fear involves punishment. The person who lives in fear doesn't have perfect love.

1 John 4:18

Financial Need

The LORD is my inheritance and my cup.
    You are the one who determines my destiny.
    Your boundary lines mark out pleasant places for
        me.
Indeed, my inheritance is something beautiful.

Psalm 16:5–6

Fear the LORD, you holy people who belong to him.
    Those who fear him are never in need.
Young lions go hungry and may starve,
    but those who seek the LORD's help have all the
        good things they need.

Psalm 34:9–10

He provides food for those who fear him.
He always remembers his promise.

Psalm 111:5

He gives food to every living creature—
    because his mercy endures forever.

Psalm 136:25

Don't ever worry and say, "What are we going to eat?" or "What are we going to drink?" or "What are we going to wear?" Everyone is concerned about these things, and your heavenly Father certainly knows you need all of them. But first, be concerned about his kingdom and what has his approval. Then all these things will be provided for you.

Matthew 6:31–33

Then Jesus said to his disciples, "So I tell you to stop worrying about what you will eat or wear. Life is more than food, and the body is more than clothes. Consider the crows. They don't plant or harvest. They don't even have a storeroom or a barn. Yet, God feeds them. You are worth much more than birds."

Luke 12:22–24

My God will richly fill your every need in a glorious way through Christ Jesus. Glory belongs to our God and Father forever! Amen.

Philippians 4:19–20

A godly life brings huge profits to people who are content with what they have. We didn't bring anything into the world, and we can't take anything out of it. As long as we have food and clothes, we should be satisfied.

1 Timothy 6:6–8

Don't love money. Be happy with what you have because God has said, "I will never abandon you or leave you." So we can confidently say,

"The Lord is my helper.
  I will not be afraid.
    What can mortals do to me?"

Hebrews 13:5–6

Grief

You have seen it; yes, you have taken note of trouble
   and grief
and placed them under your control.
   The victim entrusts himself to you.
You alone have been the helper of orphans.

Psalm 10:14

(You have kept a record of my wanderings.
   Put my tears in your bottle.
      They are already in your book.)
Then my enemies will retreat when I call to you.
This I know: God is on my side.

Psalm 56:8–9

Blessed are those who mourn.
   They will be comforted.

Matthew 5:4

Come to me, all who are tired from carrying heavy loads, and I will give you rest. Place my yoke over your shoulders, and learn from me, because I am gentle and humble. Then you will find rest for yourselves because my yoke is easy and my burden is light.

Matthew 11:28–30

I can guarantee this truth: You will cry because you are sad, but the world will be happy. You will feel pain, but your pain will turn to happiness.

John 16:20

Brothers and sisters, we don't want you to be ignorant about those who have died. We don't want you to grieve like other people who have no hope. We believe that Jesus died and came back to life. We also believe that, through Jesus, God will bring back those who have died. They will come back with Jesus.

1 Thessalonians 4:13–14

I saw a new heaven and a new earth, because the first heaven and earth had disappeared, and the sea was gone. Then I saw the holy city, New Jerusalem, coming down from God out of heaven, dressed like a bride ready for her husband. I heard a loud voice from the throne say, "God lives with humans! God will make his home with them, and they will be his people. God himself will be with them and be their God. He will wipe every tear from their eyes. There won't be any more death. There won't be any grief, crying, or pain, because the first things have disappeared."

Revelation 21:1–4

Heartache

The Lord is a stronghold for the oppressed,
a stronghold in times of trouble.
Those who know your name trust you, O Lord,
because you have never deserted those who seek
your help.

Psalm 9:9–10

The Lord is near to those whose hearts are humble.
He saves those whose spirits are crushed.
The righteous person has many troubles,
but the Lord rescues him from all of them.

Psalm 34:18–19

He is the healer of the brokenhearted.
He is the one who bandages their wounds.

Psalm 147:3

The LORD will continually guide you
 and satisfy you even in sun-baked places.
He will strengthen your bones.
 You will become like a watered garden
  and like a spring whose water does not stop
   flowing.

Isaiah 58:11

Hopelessness

Wait with hope for the LORD.
Be strong, and let your heart be courageous.
Yes, wait with hope for the LORD.

Psalm 27:14

The LORD's eyes are on those who fear him,
on those who wait with hope for his mercy.

Psalm 33:18

Why are you discouraged, my soul?
Why are you so restless?
Put your hope in God,
because I will still praise him.
He is my savior and my God.

Psalm 42:5

I wait for the LORD, my soul waits,
and with hope I wait for his word.

Psalm 130:5

Blessed are those who receive help from the God of
    Jacob.
Their hope rests on the LORD their God,
    who made heaven, earth,
        the sea, and everything in them.
The LORD remains faithful forever.

Psalm 146:5–6

Yet, the strength of those who wait with hope in the
    LORD
will be renewed.
    They will soar on wings like eagles.
        They will run and won't become weary.
        They will walk and won't grow tired.

Isaiah 40:31

May God, the source of hope, fill you with joy and
peace through your faith in him. Then you will overflow
with hope by the power of the Holy Spirit.

Romans 15:13

God wanted his people throughout the world to know
the glorious riches of this mystery—which is Christ living
in you, giving you the hope of glory.

Colossians 1:27

Therefore, your minds must be clear and ready for
action. Place your confidence completely in what God's
kindness will bring you when Jesus Christ appears again.

1 Peter 1:13

Illness

Blessed is the one who has concern for helpless
people.
The LORD will rescue him in times of trouble.
The LORD will protect him and keep him alive.
He will be blessed in the land.
Do not place him at the mercy of his
enemies.
The LORD will support him on his sickbed.
You will restore this person to health when he
is ill.

Psalm 41:1–3

My body and mind may waste away,
but God remains the foundation of my life
and my inheritance forever.

Psalm 73:26

Even when you're old, I'll take care of you.
Even when your hair turns gray, I'll support you.
I made you and will continue to care for you.
I'll support you and save you.

Isaiah 46:4

If any of you are having trouble, pray. If you are happy, sing psalms. If you are sick, call for the church leaders. Have them pray for you and anoint you with olive oil in the name of the Lord. (Prayers offered in faith will save those who are sick, and the Lord will cure them.) If you have sinned, you will be forgiven.

James 5:13–15

Insecurity

I fall asleep in peace the moment I lie down
   because you alone, O Lord, enable me to live
      securely.

Psalm 4:8

You bless righteous people, O Lord.
Like a large shield, you surround them with your
   favor.

Psalm 5:12

The Lord is a stronghold for the oppressed,
   a stronghold in times of trouble.
Those who know your name trust you, O Lord,
   because you have never deserted those who seek
      your help.

Psalm 9:9–10

I always keep the Lord in front of me.
   When he is by my side, I cannot be moved.
      That is why my heart is glad and my soul
         rejoices.
      My body rests securely.

Psalm 16:8–9

He will never fail.
A righteous person will always be remembered.
  He is not afraid of bad news.
  His heart remains secure, full of confidence in the
    Lord.
  His heart is steady, and he is not afraid.
    In the end he will look triumphantly at his
      enemies.

Psalm 112:6–8

In the fear of the Lord there is strong confidence,
  and his children will have a place of refuge.

Proverbs 14:26

The name of the Lord is a strong tower.
  A righteous person runs to it and is safe.

Proverbs 18:10

My sheep respond to my voice, and I know who they
are. They follow me, and I give them eternal life. They will
never be lost, and no one will tear them away from me. My
Father, who gave them to me, is greater than everyone else,
and no one can tear them away from my Father.

John 10:27–29

Now, dear children, live in Christ. Then, when he appears we will have confidence, and when he comes we won't
turn from him in shame. If you know that Christ has God's
approval, you also know that everyone who does what God
approves of has been born from God.

1 John 2:28–29

Loneliness

The God who is in his holy dwelling place
   is the father of the fatherless and the defender of
      widows.
God places lonely people in families.
   He leads prisoners out of prison into productive
      lives,
      but rebellious people must live in an unproduc-
         tive land.

Psalm 68:5–6

Yet, I am always with you.
   You hold on to my right hand.

Psalm 73:23

As long as I have you,
   I don't need anyone else in heaven or on earth.
My body and mind may waste away,
   but God remains the foundation of my life
      and my inheritance forever.

Psalm 73:25–26

Whoever lives under the shelter of the Most High
will remain in the shadow of the Almighty.
I will say to the LORD,
"You are my refuge and my fortress, my God in
whom I trust."

Psalm 91:1–2

I will not leave you all alone. I will come back to you.

John 14:18

Rejection

Those who know your name trust you, O Lord,
because you have never deserted those who seek
your help.

Psalm 9:10

Even if my father and mother abandon me,
the Lord will take care of me.

Psalm 27:10

The Lord will never desert his people
or abandon those who belong to him.

Psalm 94:14

Whoever does what God wants is my brother and sister
and mother.

Mark 3:35

Blessed are you when people hate you, avoid you,
insult you, and slander you
because you are committed to the Son of Man.

Luke 6:22

The person who hears you hears me, and the person who rejects you rejects me. The person who rejects me rejects the one who sent me.

Luke 10:16

Everyone whom the Father gives me will come to me. I will never turn away anyone who comes to me.

John 6:37

Who will accuse those whom God has chosen? God has approved of them. Who will condemn them? Christ has died, and more importantly, he was brought back to life. Christ has the highest position in heaven. Christ also intercedes for us.

Romans 8:33–34

His favor is with everyone who has an undying love for our Lord Jesus Christ.

Ephesians 6:24

As a result, God in his kindness has given us his approval and we have become heirs who have the confidence that we have everlasting life.

Titus 3:7

Repentance

However, if my people, who are called by my name,
    will humble themselves,
        pray, search for me, and turn from their evil ways,
            then I will hear their prayer from heaven,
                forgive their sins,
    and heal their country.

2 Chronicles 7:14

This is what the Almighty LORD, the Holy One of
    Israel, says:
You can be saved by returning to me.
You can have rest.
You can be strong by being quiet and by trusting me.
    But you don't want that.

Isaiah 30:15

Let wicked people abandon their ways.
Let evil people abandon their thoughts.
Let them return to the LORD,
    and he will show compassion to them.
Let them return to our God,
    because he will freely forgive them.

Isaiah 55:7

I can guarantee that there will be more happiness in heaven over one person who turns to God and changes the way he thinks and acts than over 99 people who already have turned to God and have his approval.

Luke 15:7

So change the way you think and act, and turn to God to have your sins removed.

Acts 3:19

Don't become like the people of this world. Instead, change the way you think. Then you will always be able to determine what God really wants—what is good, pleasing, and perfect.

Romans 12:2

In fact, to be distressed in a godly way causes people to change the way they think and act and leads them to be saved. No one can regret that. But the distress that the world causes brings only death.

2 Corinthians 7:10

The Lord isn't slow to do what he promised, as some people think. Rather, he is patient for your sake. He doesn't want to destroy anyone but wants all people to have an opportunity to turn to him and change the way they think and act.

2 Peter 3:9

God is faithful and reliable. If we confess our sins, he forgives them and cleanses us from everything we've done wrong.

1 John 1:9

I correct and discipline everyone I love. Take this seriously, and change the way you think and act.

Revelation 3:19

Self-Centeredness

Direct my heart toward your written instructions
    rather than getting rich in underhanded ways.
Turn my eyes away from worthless things.
Give me a new life in your ways.

Psalm 119:36–37

Whoever has pity on the poor lends to the LORD,
    and he will repay him for his good deed.

Proverbs 19:17

Love each other as I have loved you. This is what I'm commanding you to do. The greatest love you can show is to give your life for your friends. You are my friends if you obey my commandments.

John 15:12–14

Love is patient. Love is kind. Love isn't jealous. It doesn't sing its own praises. It isn't arrogant. It isn't rude. It doesn't think about itself. It isn't irritable. It doesn't keep track of wrongs.

1 Corinthians 13:4–5

You were indeed called to be free, brothers and sisters. Don't turn this freedom into an excuse for your corrupt nature to express itself. Rather, serve each other through love. All of Moses' Teachings are summarized in a single statement, "Love your neighbor as you love yourself." But if you criticize and attack each other, be careful that you don't destroy each other.

Galatians 5:13–15

Don't act out of selfish ambition or be conceited. Instead, humbly think of others as being better than yourselves. Don't be concerned only about your own interests, but also be concerned about the interests of others.

Philippians 2:3–4

But if you are bitterly jealous and filled with self-centered ambition, don't brag. Don't say that you are wise when it isn't true. That kind of wisdom doesn't come from above. It belongs to this world. It is self-centered and demonic. Wherever there is jealousy and rivalry, there is disorder and every kind of evil.

However, the wisdom that comes from above is first of all pure. Then it is peaceful, gentle, obedient, filled with mercy and good deeds, impartial, and sincere. A harvest that has God's approval comes from the peace planted by peacemakers.

James 3:14–18

We understand what love is when we realize that Christ gave his life for us. That means we must give our lives for other believers. Now, suppose a person has enough to live on and notices another believer in need. How can God's love be in that person if he doesn't bother to help the other believer?

1 John 3:16–17

Stress

The LORD is my shepherd.
   I am never in need.
      He makes me lie down in green pastures.
      He leads me beside peaceful waters.
      He renews my soul.
      He guides me along the paths of righteousness
         for the sake of his name.
Even though I walk through the dark valley of
      death,
   because you are with me, I fear no harm.
      Your rod and your staff give me courage.

Psalm 23:1–4

Every path of the LORD is one of mercy and truth
   for those who cling to his promise and written
      instructions.

Psalm 25:10

The LORD will be your confidence.
He will keep your foot from getting caught.

Proverbs 3:26

With perfect peace you will protect those whose
    minds cannot be changed,
  because they trust you.
Trust the LORD always,
  because the LORD, the LORD alone, is an everlast-
    ing rock.

Isaiah 26:3–4

This is what the Almighty LORD says:
I am going to lay a rock in Zion,
  a rock that has been tested,
  a precious cornerstone,
  a solid foundation.
    Whoever believes in him will not worry.

Isaiah 28:16

This is what the Almighty LORD, the Holy One of
    Israel, says:
You can be saved by returning to me.
You can have rest.
You can be strong by being quiet and by trusting me.
  But you don't want that.

Isaiah 30:15

Come to me, all who are tired from carrying heavy loads,
and I will give you rest. Place my yoke over your shoulders,
and learn from me, because I am gentle and humble. Then
you will find rest for yourselves because my yoke is easy
and my burden is light.

Matthew 11:28–30

Never worry about anything. But in every situation let God know what you need in prayers and requests while giving thanks. Then God's peace, which goes beyond anything we can imagine, will guard your thoughts and emotions through Christ Jesus.

Philippians 4:6–7

Trial

You are my hiding place.
You protect me from trouble.
You surround me with joyous songs of salvation.

Psalm 32:7

The righteous person has many troubles,
but the LORD rescues him from all of them.

Psalm 34:19

Because you love me, I will rescue you.
I will protect you because you know my name.
When you call to me, I will answer you.
I will be with you when you are in trouble.
I will save you and honor you.

Psalm 91:14–15

Even though I walk into the middle of trouble,
you guard my life against the anger of my
enemies.
You stretch out your hand,
and your right hand saves me.

Psalm 138:7

I've told you this so that my peace will be with you. In the world you'll have trouble. But cheer up! I have overcome the world.

John 16:33

There isn't any temptation that you have experienced which is unusual for humans. God, who faithfully keeps his promises, will not allow you to be tempted beyond your power to resist. But when you are tempted, he will also give you the ability to endure the temptation as your way of escape.

1 Corinthians 10:13

My brothers and sisters, be very happy when you are tested in different ways.

James 1:2

Blessed are those who endure when they are tested. When they pass the test, they will receive the crown of life that God has promised to those who love him.

James 1:12

Dear friends, don't be surprised by the fiery troubles that are coming in order to test you. Don't feel as though something strange is happening to you, but be happy as you share Christ's sufferings. Then you will also be full of joy when he appears again in his glory. If you are insulted because of the name of Christ, you are blessed because the Spirit of glory—the Spirit of God—is resting on you.

1 Peter 4:12–14

Since the Lord did all this, he knows how to rescue godly people when they are tested. He also knows how to hold immoral people for punishment on the day of judgment.

2 Peter 2:9

Uncertainty about the Future

Horses are not a guarantee for victory.
    Their great strength cannot help someone escape.
The LORD's eyes are on those who fear him,
    on those who wait with hope for his mercy
        to rescue their souls from death
            and keep them alive during a famine.
We wait for the LORD.
    He is our help and our shield.
    In him our hearts find joy.
    In his holy name we trust.
Let your mercy rest on us, O LORD,
    since we wait with hope for you.

Psalm 33:17–22

Trust the LORD with all your heart,
    and do not rely on your own understanding.
In all your ways acknowledge him,
    and he will make your paths smooth.

Proverbs 3:5–6

Whoever gives attention to the LORD's word
prospers,
and blessed is the person who trusts the LORD.

Proverbs 16:20

Trust the LORD always,
because the LORD, the Lord alone, is an everlasting rock.

Isaiah 26:4

I know the plans that I have for you, declares the LORD. They are plans for peace and not disaster, plans to give you a future filled with hope.

Jeremiah 29:11

Don't be troubled. Believe in God, and believe in me. My Father's house has many rooms. If that were not true, would I have told you that I'm going to prepare a place for you? If I go to prepare a place for you, I will come again. Then I will bring you into my presence so that you will be where I am.

John 14:1–3

God Promises to Meet
Women's Need for . . .

Acceptance

The LORD your God is a merciful God. He will not abandon you, destroy you, or forget the promise to your ancestors that he swore he would keep.

Deuteronomy 4:31

For the sake of his great name, the LORD will not abandon his people, because the LORD wants to make you his people.

1 Samuel 12:22

May the LORD our God be with us as he was with our ancestors. May he never leave us or abandon us.

1 Kings 8:57

Even if my father and mother abandon me,
    the LORD will take care of me.

Psalm 27:10

The Lord is your guardian.
The Lord is the shade over your right hand.
    The sun will not beat down on you during the day,
        nor will the moon at night.
The Lord guards you from every evil.
    He guards your life.
The Lord guards you as you come and go,
    now and forever.

Psalm 121:5–8

Every word of God has proven to be true.
    He is a shield to those who come to him for
        protection.

Proverbs 30:5

The Lord is good.
    He is a fortress in the day of trouble.
    He knows those who seek shelter in him.

Nahum 1:7

However, he gave the right to become God's children to everyone who believed in him.

John 1:12

Everyone whom the Father gives me will come to me. I will never turn away anyone who comes to me.

John 6:37

Who will accuse those whom God has chosen? God has approved of them. Who will condemn them? Christ has died, and more importantly, he was brought back to life. Christ has the highest position in heaven. Christ also intercedes for us.

Romans 8:33–34

Therefore, accept each other in the same way that Christ accepted you. He did this to bring glory to God.

Romans 15:7

There are neither Jews nor Greeks, slaves nor free people, males nor females. You are all the same in Christ Jesus.

Galatians 3:28

Assurance

Those who trust the LORD are like Mount Zion,
which can never be shaken.
It remains firm forever.
As the mountains surround Jerusalem,
so the LORD surrounds his people now and
forever.

Psalm 125:1–2

The child will become the shepherd of his flock.
He will lead them with the strength of the LORD,
with the majestic name of the LORD his God.
They will live in safety
because his greatness will reach the ends of the
earth.

Micah 5:4

As Moses lifted up the snake on a pole in the desert,
so the Son of Man must be lifted up. Then everyone who
believes in him will have eternal life.

John 3:14–15

I can guarantee this truth: Those who listen to what I say and believe in the one who sent me will have eternal life. They won't be judged because they have already passed from death to life.

John 5:24

Everyone whom the Father gives me will come to me. I will never turn away anyone who comes to me. I haven't come from heaven to do what I want to do. I've come to do what the one who sent me wants me to do. The one who sent me doesn't want me to lose any of those he gave me. He wants me to bring them back to life on the last day.

John 6:37–39

My sheep respond to my voice, and I know who they are. They follow me, and I give them eternal life. They will never be lost, and no one will tear them away from me. My Father, who gave them to me, is greater than everyone else, and no one can tear them away from my Father.

John 10:27–29

I am convinced that nothing can ever separate us from God's love which Christ Jesus our Lord shows us. We can't be separated by death or life, by angels or rulers, by anything in the present or anything in the future, by forces or powers in the world above or in the world below, or by anything else in creation.

Romans 8:38–39

You heard and believed the message of truth, the Good News that he has saved you. In him you were sealed with the Holy Spirit whom he promised. This Holy Spirit is the guarantee that we will receive our inheritance. We have this guarantee until we are set free to belong to him. God receives praise and glory for this.

Ephesians 1:13–14

I'm convinced that God, who began this good work in you, will carry it through to completion on the day of Christ Jesus.

Philippians 1:6

But the Lord is faithful and will strengthen you and protect you against the evil one.

2 Thessalonians 3:3

For this reason I suffer as I do. However, I'm not ashamed. I know whom I trust. I'm convinced that he is able to protect what he had entrusted to me until that day.

2 Timothy 1:12

We have this confidence as a sure and strong anchor for our lives. This confidence goes into the holy place behind the curtain where Jesus went before us on our behalf. He has become the chief priest forever in the way Melchizedek was a priest.

Hebrews 6:19–20

Brothers and sisters, because of the blood of Jesus we can now confidently go into the holy place. Jesus has opened a new and living way for us to go through the curtain. (The curtain is his own body.) We have a superior priest in charge of God's house. We have been sprinkled with his blood to free us from a guilty conscience, and our bodies have been washed with clean water. So we must continue to come to him with a sincere heart and strong faith.

Hebrews 10:19–22

Whenever our conscience condemns us, we will be reassured that God is greater than our conscience and knows everything.

1 John 3:20

Blessing

You bless righteous people, O Lord.
Like a large shield, you surround them with your
    favor.

Psalm 5:12

Your kindness is so great!
    You reserve it for those who fear you.
        Adam's descendants watch
            as you show it to those who take refuge in
            you.

Psalm 31:19

Blessed is the person you choose
    and invite to live with you in your courtyards.
        We will be filled with good food from your
            house,
            from your holy temple.

Psalm 65:4

Blessed are all who fear the LORD
  and live his way.
You will certainly eat what your own hands have
    provided.
  Blessings to you!
  May things go well for you!

Psalm 128:1–2

Blessings cover the head of a righteous person,
  but violence covers the mouths of wicked people.

Proverbs 10:6

Jesus looked at his disciples and said,
"Blessed are those who are poor.
  The kingdom of God is theirs.
Blessed are those who are hungry.
  They will be satisfied.
Blessed are those who are crying.
  They will laugh.
Blessed are you when people hate you, avoid you,
  insult you, and slander you
    because you are committed to the Son of Man.
      Rejoice then, and be very happy!
        You have a great reward in heaven.
          That's the way their ancestors treated
            the prophets."

Luke 6:20–23

There is no difference between Jews and Greeks. They all have the same Lord, who gives his riches to everyone who calls on him.

Romans 10:12

Praise the God and Father of our Lord Jesus Christ! Through Christ, God has blessed us with every spiritual blessing that heaven has to offer.

Ephesians 1:3

Children, obey your parents because you are Christians. This is the right thing to do. "Honor your father and mother that everything may go well for you, and you may have a long life on earth." This is an important commandment with a promise.

Ephesians 6:1–3

Comfort

The Lord is near to those whose hearts are humble.
He saves those whose spirits are crushed.

Psalm 34:18

As I lie on my bed, I remember you.
   Through the long hours of the night, I think
      about you.
You have been my help.
   In the shadow of your wings, I sing joyfully.
My soul clings to you.
   Your right hand supports me.

Psalm 63:6–8

Grant me some proof of your goodness
   so that those who hate me may see it and be put
      to shame.
You, O Lord, have helped me and comforted me.

Psalm 86:17

This is my comfort in my misery:
   Your promise gave me a new life.

Psalm 119:50

He is the healer of the brokenhearted.
He is the one who bandages their wounds.

Psalm 147:3

Blessed are those who mourn.
They will be comforted.

Matthew 5:4

Come to me, all who are tired from carrying heavy loads, and I will give you rest. Place my yoke over your shoulders, and learn from me, because I am gentle and humble. Then you will find rest for yourselves because my yoke is easy and my burden is light.

Matthew 11:28–30

Don't be troubled. Believe in God, and believe in me. My Father's house has many rooms. If that were not true, would I have told you that I'm going to prepare a place for you? If I go to prepare a place for you, I will come again. Then I will bring you into my presence so that you will be where I am.

John 14:1–3

Praise the God and Father of our Lord Jesus Christ! He is the Father who is compassionate and the God who gives comfort. He comforts us whenever we suffer. That is why whenever other people suffer, we are able to comfort them by using the same comfort we have received from God.

2 Corinthians 1:3–4

God our Father loved us and by his kindness gave us everlasting encouragement and good hope. Together with our Lord Jesus Christ, may he encourage and strengthen you to do and say everything that is good.

2 Thessalonians 2:16–17

The lamb in the center near the throne will be their shepherd.
He will lead them to springs filled with the water of life,
    and God will wipe every tear from their eyes.

Revelation 7:17

Compassion

But you, O Lord, are a compassionate and merciful
   God.
   You are patient, always faithful and ready to
      forgive.

Psalm 86:15

As a father has compassion for his children,
   so the LORD has compassion for those who fear
      him.

Psalm 103:13

He has made his miracles unforgettable.
   The LORD is merciful and compassionate.
He provides food for those who fear him.
He always remembers his promise.

Psalm 111:4–5

The LORD is merciful and righteous.
Our God is compassionate.
The LORD protects defenseless people.
   When I was weak, he saved me.

Psalm 116:5–6

The LORD is waiting to be kind to you.
He rises to have compassion on you.
The LORD is a God of justice.
Blessed are all those who wait for him.

Isaiah 30:18

Sing with joy, you heavens!
Rejoice, you earth!
Break into shouts of joy, you mountains!
The LORD has comforted his people
and will have compassion on his humble
people.

Isaiah 49:13

"The mountains may move, and the hills may shake,
but my kindness will never depart from you.
My promise of peace will never change,"
says the LORD, who has compassion on you.

Isaiah 54:10

I love you with an everlasting love.
So I will continue to show you my kindness.

Jeremiah 31:3

The reason I can still find hope is that I keep this one
thing in mind:
the LORD's mercy.
We were not completely wiped out.
His compassion is never limited.
It is new every morning.
His faithfulness is great.

Lamentations 3:21–23

Praise the God and Father of our Lord Jesus Christ! He is the Father who is compassionate and the God who gives comfort.

2 Corinthians 1:3

God our Father loved us and by his kindness gave us everlasting encouragement and good hope. Together with our Lord Jesus Christ, may he encourage and strengthen you to do and say everything that is good.

2 Thessalonians 2:16–17

My child, find your source of strength in the kindness of Christ Jesus.

2 Timothy 2:1

Encouragement

You have heard the desire of oppressed people,
  O Lord.
You encourage them.
You pay close attention to them.

Psalm 10:17

I believe that I will see the goodness of the Lord
  in this world of the living.
Wait with hope for the Lord.
Be strong, and let your heart be courageous.
Yes, wait with hope for the Lord.

Psalm 27:13–14

Why are you discouraged, my soul?
Why are you so restless?
  Put your hope in God,
    because I will still praise him.
      He is my savior and my God.

Psalm 42:5

Praise the Lord, my soul,
  and never forget all the good he has done:
    He is the one who forgives all your sins,

the one who heals all your diseases,
the one who rescues your life from the pit,
the one who crowns you with mercy and
    compassion,
the one who fills your life with blessings
  so that you become young again like an
    eagle.

Psalm 103:2–5

I'm leaving you peace. I'm giving you my peace. I don't give you the kind of peace that the world gives. So don't be troubled or cowardly. You heard me tell you, "I'm going away, but I'm coming back to you." If you loved me, you would be glad that I'm going to the Father, because the Father is greater than I am.

John 14:27–28

Everything written long ago was written to teach us so that we would have confidence through the endurance and encouragement which the Scriptures give us.

Romans 15:4

God our Father loved us and by his kindness gave us everlasting encouragement and good hope. Together with our Lord Jesus Christ, may he encourage and strengthen you to do and say everything that is good.

2 Thessalonians 2:16–17

We have this confidence as a sure and strong anchor for our lives. This confidence goes into the holy place behind the curtain where Jesus went before us on our behalf. He has become the chief priest forever in the way Melchizedek was a priest.

Hebrews 6:19–20

Fellowship

See how good and pleasant it is
  when brothers and sisters live together in
    harmony!
  It is like fine, scented oil on the head,
    running down the beard—down Aaron's
      beard—
    running over the collar of his robes.
  It is like dew on Mount Hermon,
    dew which comes down on Zion's
      mountains.
    That is where the LORD promised
      the blessing of eternal life.

Psalm 133

Where two or three have come together in my name, I am there among them.

Matthew 18:20

I'm giving you a new commandment: Love each other in the same way that I have loved you. Everyone will know that you are my disciples because of your love for each other.

John 13:34–35

I will not leave you all alone. I will come back to you. In a little while the world will no longer see me, but you will see me. You will live because I live. On that day you will know that I am in my Father and that you are in me and that I am in you.

John 14:18–20

We must also consider how to encourage each other to show love and to do good things. We should not stop gathering together with other believers, as some of you are doing. Instead, we must continue to encourage each other even more as we see the day of the Lord coming.

Hebrews 10:24–25

Finally, everyone must live in harmony, be sympathetic, love each other, have compassion, and be humble. Don't pay people back with evil for the evil they do to you, or ridicule those who ridicule you. Instead, bless them, because you were called to inherit a blessing.

1 Peter 3:8–9

This is the life we have seen and heard. We are reporting about it to you also so that you, too, can have a relationship with us. Our relationship is with the Father and with his Son Jesus Christ.

1 John 1:3

But if we live in the light in the same way that God is in the light, we have a relationship with each other. And the blood of his Son Jesus cleanses us from every sin.

1 John 1:7

Forgiveness

Blessed is the person whose disobedience is forgiven
   and whose sin is pardoned.
Blessed is the person whom the LORD no longer
      accuses of sin
   and who has no deceitful thoughts.

Psalm 32:1–2

Purify me from sin with hyssop, and I will be clean.
Wash me, and I will be whiter than snow.

Psalm 51:7

Various sins overwhelm me.
   You are the one who forgives our rebellious acts.

Psalm 65:3

As far as the east is from the west—
   that is how far he has removed our rebellious acts
      from himself.

Psalm 103:12

O Lord, who would be able to stand
  if you kept a record of sins?
But with you there is forgiveness
  so that you can be feared.

Psalm 130:3–4

"Come on now, let's discuss this!" says the Lord.
"Though your sins are bright red,
  they will become as white as snow.
Though they are dark red,
  they will become as white as wool."

Isaiah 1:18

Whenever you pray, forgive anything you have against anyone. Then your Father in heaven will forgive your failures.

Mark 11:25

Peter answered them, "All of you must turn to God and change the way you think and act, and each of you must be baptized in the name of Jesus Christ so that your sins will be forgiven. Then you will receive the Holy Spirit as a gift. This promise belongs to you and to your children and to everyone who is far away. It belongs to everyone who worships the Lord our God."

Acts 2:38–39

Through the blood of his Son, we are set free from our sins. God forgives our failures because of his overflowing kindness. He poured out his kindness by giving us every kind of wisdom and insight when he revealed the mystery of his plan to us. He had decided to do this through Christ.

Ephesians 1:7–9

God has rescued us from the power of darkness and has brought us into the kingdom of his Son, whom he loves. His Son paid the price to free us, which means that our sins are forgiven.

Colossians 1:13–14

You were once dead because of your failures and your uncircumcised corrupt nature. But God made you alive with Christ when he forgave all our failures. He did this by erasing the charges that were brought against us by the written laws God had established. He took the charges away by nailing them to the cross.

Colossians 2:13–14

If any of you are having trouble, pray. If you are happy, sing psalms. If you are sick, call for the church leaders. Have them pray for you and anoint you with olive oil in the name of the Lord. (Prayers offered in faith will save those who are sick, and the Lord will cure them.) If you have sinned, you will be forgiven. So admit your sins to each other, and pray for each other so that you will be healed.

James 5:13–16

God is faithful and reliable. If we confess our sins, he forgives them and cleanses us from everything we've done wrong.

1 John 1:9

Grace

Then he passed in front of Moses, calling out, "The LORD, the LORD, a compassionate and merciful God, patient, always faithful and ready to forgive."

Exodus 34:6

He has made his miracles unforgettable.
The LORD is merciful and compassionate.

Psalm 111:4

The LORD is merciful, compassionate, patient,
and always ready to forgive.

Psalm 145:8

When he mocks the mockers,
he is gracious to humble people.

Proverbs 3:34

You know about the kindness of our Lord Jesus Christ. He was rich, yet for your sake he became poor in order to make you rich through his poverty.

2 Corinthians 8:9

Besides, God will give you his constantly overflowing kindness. Then, when you always have everything you need, you can do more and more good things.

2 Corinthians 9:8

But he told me: "My kindness is all you need. My power is strongest when you are weak." So I will brag even more about my weaknesses in order that Christ's power will live in me.

2 Corinthians 12:9

God saved you through faith as an act of kindness. You had nothing to do with it. Being saved is a gift from God. It's not the result of anything you've done, so no one can brag about it. God has made us what we are. He has created us in Christ Jesus to live lives filled with good works that he has prepared for us to do.

Ephesians 2:8–10

God saved us and called us to be holy, not because of what we had done, but because of his own plan and kindness. Before the world began, God planned that Christ Jesus would show us God's kindness.

2 Timothy 1:9

So we can go confidently to the throne of God's kindness to receive mercy and find kindness, which will help us at the right time.

Hebrews 4:16

God, who shows you his kindness and who has called you through Christ Jesus to his eternal glory, will restore you, strengthen you, make you strong, and support you as you suffer for a little while.

1 Peter 5:10

Identity

Come, let's worship and bow down.
Let's kneel in front of the LORD, our maker,
because he is our God
and we are the people in his care,
the flock that he leads.

Psalm 95:6–7

Realize that the LORD alone is God.
He made us, and we are his.
We are his people and the sheep in his care.

Psalm 100:3

My sheep respond to my voice, and I know who they are. They follow me, and I give them eternal life. They will never be lost, and no one will tear them away from me. My Father, who gave them to me, is greater than everyone else, and no one can tear them away from my Father.

John 10:27–29

This is true because he already knew his people and had already appointed them to have the same form as the image of his Son. Therefore, his Son is the firstborn among many children. He also called those whom he had already appointed. He approved of those whom he had called, and he gave glory to those whom he had approved of.

Romans 8:29–30

> Those who are not my people
>   I will call my people.
> Those who are not loved
>   I will call my loved ones.
> Wherever they were told,
>   "You are not my people,"
>   they will be called children of the living God.

Romans 9:25–26

You belong to Christ, and Christ belongs to God.

1 Corinthians 3:23

But when the right time came, God sent his Son into the world. A woman gave birth to him, and he came under the control of the laws given to Moses. God sent him to pay for the freedom of those who were controlled by these laws so that we would be adopted as his children. Because you are God's children, God has sent the Spirit of his Son into us to call out, "Abba! Father!" So you are no longer slaves but God's children. Since you are God's children, God has also made you heirs.

Galatians 4:4–7

You heard and believed the message of truth, the Good News that he has saved you. In him you were sealed with the Holy Spirit whom he promised. This Holy Spirit is the guarantee that we will receive our inheritance. We have this guarantee until we are set free to belong to him. God receives praise and glory for this.

Ephesians 1:13–14

As a result, God in his kindness has given us his approval and we have become heirs who have the confidence that we have everlasting life.

Titus 3:7

Endure your discipline. God corrects you as a father corrects his children. All children are disciplined by their fathers.

Hebrews 12:7

However, you are chosen people, a royal priesthood, a holy nation, people who belong to God. You were chosen to tell about the excellent qualities of God, who called you out of darkness into his marvelous light.

1 Peter 2:9

Consider this: The Father has given us his love. He loves us so much that we are actually called God's dear children. And that's what we are. For this reason the world doesn't recognize us, and it didn't recognize him either. Dear friends, now we are God's children. What we will be isn't completely clear yet. We do know that when Christ appears we will be like him because we will see him as he is.

1 John 3:1–2

Everyone who wins the victory this way will wear white clothes. I will never erase their names from the Book of Life. I will acknowledge them in the presence of my Father and his angels.

Revelation 3:5

Justice

Entrust your ways to the Lord.
Trust him, and he will act on your behalf.
  He will make your righteousness shine like a light,
    your just cause like the noonday sun.

Psalm 37:5–6

He has reserved priceless wisdom for decent people.
He is a shield for those who walk in integrity
  in order to guard those on paths of justice
    and to watch over the way of his godly ones.

Proverbs 2:7–8

Many seek an audience with a ruler,
  but justice for humanity comes from the Lord.

Proverbs 29:26

The Lord is waiting to be kind to you.
He rises to have compassion on you.
  The Lord is a God of justice.
    Blessed are all those who wait for him.

Isaiah 30:18

God showed that Christ is the throne of mercy where God's approval is given through faith in Christ's blood. In his patience God waited to deal with sins committed in the past. He waited so that he could display his approval at the present time. This shows that he is a God of justice, a God who approves of people who believe in Jesus.

Romans 3:25–26

Life

You make the path of life known to me.
  Complete joy is in your presence.
    Pleasures are by your side forever.

                        Psalm 16:11

Indeed, the fountain of life is with you.
  In your light we see light.

                        Psalm 36:9

  He guards your life.
The Lord guards you as you come and go,
  now and forever.

                        Psalm 121:7–8

My son,
  listen and accept my words,
    and they will multiply the years of your life.
      I have taught you the way of wisdom.
      I have guided you along decent paths.
        When you walk, your stride will not be
          hampered.
          Even if you run, you will not stumble.

                        Proverbs 4:10–12

The fear of the LORD lengthens the number of days, but the years of wicked people are shortened.

Proverbs 10:27

Jesus told them, "I am the bread of life. Whoever comes to me will never become hungry, and whoever believes in me will never become thirsty."

John 6:35

A thief comes to steal, kill, and destroy. But I came so that my sheep will have life and so that they will have everything they need.

John 10:10

It is certain that death ruled because of one person's failure. It's even more certain that those who receive God's overflowing kindness and the gift of his approval will rule in life because of one person, Jesus Christ.

Romans 5:17

Does the Spirit of the one who brought Jesus back to life live in you? Then the one who brought Christ back to life will also make your mortal bodies alive by his Spirit who lives in you.

Romans 8:11

Since you were brought back to life with Christ, focus on the things that are above—where Christ holds the highest position. Keep your mind on things above, not on worldly things. You have died, and your life is hidden with Christ in God. Christ is your life. When he appears, then you, too, will appear with him in glory.

Colossians 3:1–4

Praise the God and Father of our Lord Jesus Christ! God has given us a new birth because of his great mercy. We have been born into a new life that has a confidence which is alive because Jesus Christ has come back to life.

1 Peter 1:3

Protection

Even though I walk through the dark valley of
    death,
    because you are with me, I fear no harm.
        Your rod and your staff give me courage.

Psalm 23:4

The victory for righteous people comes from the
    Lord.
    He is their fortress in times of trouble.
The Lord helps them and rescues them.
He rescues them from wicked people.
He saves them because they have taken refuge in
    him.

Psalm 37:39–40

You, O Lord, are my refuge!
You have made the Most High your home.
    No harm will come to you.
    No sickness will come near your house.
He will put his angels in charge of you
    to protect you in all your ways.

Psalm 91:9–11

The Lord guards you from every evil.
  He guards your life.
The Lord guards you as you come and go,
  now and forever.

Psalm 121:7–8

Every word of God has proven to be true.
  He is a shield to those who come to him for
    protection.

Proverbs 30:5

Don't be afraid, because I am with you.
Don't be intimidated; I am your God.
  I will strengthen you.
  I will help you.
  I will support you with my victorious right hand.

Isaiah 41:10

The one who loves us gives us an overwhelming victory in all these difficulties. I am convinced that nothing can ever separate us from God's love which Christ Jesus our Lord shows us. We can't be separated by death or life, by angels or rulers, by anything in the present or anything in the future, by forces or powers in the world above or in the world below, or by anything else in creation.

Romans 8:37–39

But the Lord is faithful and will strengthen you and protect you against the evil one.

2 Thessalonians 3:3

We know that those who have been born from God don't go on sinning. Rather, the Son of God protects them, and the evil one can't harm them.

1 John 5:18

God can guard you so that you don't fall and so that you can be full of joy as you stand in his glorious presence without fault.

Jude 24

Quiet and Peace

The LORD is my shepherd.
   I am never in need.
      He makes me lie down in green pastures.
      He leads me beside peaceful waters.

Psalm 23:1–2

The LORD will give power to his people.
The LORD will bless his people with peace.

Psalm 29:11

My soul waits calmly for God alone.
   My salvation comes from him.
He alone is my rock and my savior—my stronghold.
   I cannot be severely shaken.

Psalm 62:1–2

Whoever lives under the shelter of the Most High
   will remain in the shadow of the Almighty.

Psalm 91:1

Instead, I have kept my soul calm and quiet.
My soul is content as a weaned child is content in
its mother's arms.

Psalm 131:2

With perfect peace you will protect those whose
minds cannot be changed,
because they trust you.

Isaiah 26:3

The Lord is good to those who wait for him,
to anyone who seeks help from him.
It is good to continue to hope and wait silently
for the Lord to save us.

Lamentations 3:25–26

I'm leaving you peace. I'm giving you my peace. I don't give you the kind of peace that the world gives. So don't be troubled or cowardly.

John 14:27

I've told you this so that my peace will be with you. In the world you'll have trouble. But cheer up! I have overcome the world.

John 16:33

First of all, I encourage you to make petitions, prayers, intercessions, and prayers of thanks for all people, for rulers, and for everyone who has authority over us. Pray for these people so that we can have a quiet and peaceful life always lived in a godly and reverent way. This is good and pleases God our Savior. He wants all people to be saved and to learn the truth.

1 Timothy 2:1–4

However, the wisdom that comes from above is first of all pure. Then it is peaceful, gentle, obedient, filled with mercy and good deeds, impartial, and sincere. A harvest that has God's approval comes from the peace planted by peacemakers.

James 3:17–18

Renewal

He renews my soul.
He guides me along the paths of righteousness
    for the sake of his name.

Psalm 23:3

Create a clean heart in me, O God,
    and renew a faithful spirit within me.

Psalm 51:10

The High and Lofty One lives forever, and his name
    is holy.
This is what he says:
I live in a high and holy place.
    But I am with those who are crushed and humble.
        I will renew the spirit of those who are humble
            and the courage of those who are crushed.

Isaiah 57:15

I will give you a new heart and put a new spirit in you.
I will remove your stubborn hearts and give you obedient
hearts. I will put my Spirit in you. I will enable you to live
by my laws, and you will obey my rules.

Ezekiel 36:26–27

"Do not be afraid, Zion!
Do not lose courage!"
The LORD your God is with you.
He is a hero who saves you.
He happily rejoices over you,
renews you with his love,
and celebrates over you with shouts of joy.

Zephaniah 3:16–17

However, you were taught to have a new attitude.

Ephesians 4:23

Don't lie to each other. You've gotten rid of the person you used to be and the life you used to live, and you've become a new person. This new person is continually renewed in knowledge to be like its Creator.

Colossians 3:9–10

True Success

Blessed is the person who does not
    follow the advice of wicked people,
       take the path of sinners,
          or join the company of mockers.
Rather, he delights in the teachings of the LORD
    and reflects on his teachings day and night.
He is like a tree planted beside streams—
    a tree that produces fruit in season
      and whose leaves do not wither.
He succeeds in everything he does.

                            Psalm 1:1–3

O LORD, you light my lamp.
    My God turns my darkness into light.
       With you I can attack a line of soldiers.
       With my God I can break through barricades.

                        Psalm 18:28–29

Some rely on chariots and others on horses,
    but we will boast in the name of the LORD our
       God.
       They will sink to their knees and fall,
       but we will rise and stand firm.

                        Psalm 20:7–8

Hallelujah!
Blessed is the person who fears the Lord
    and is happy to obey his commands.
        His descendants will grow strong on the earth.
        The family of a decent person will be blessed.
            Wealth and riches will be in his home.
            His righteousness continues forever.

Psalm 112:1–3

Entrust your efforts to the Lord,
    and your plans will succeed.

Proverbs 16:3

We know that all things work together for the good of those who love God—those whom he has called according to his plan.

Romans 8:28

My brothers and sisters, be very happy when you are tested in different ways. You know that such testing of your faith produces endurance. Endure until your testing is over. Then you will be mature and complete, and you won't need anything.

James 1:2–4

Who wins the victory over the world? Isn't it the person who believes that Jesus is the Son of God?

1 John 5:5

God Promises to Help
Women Grow in . . .

Attitude

Come, let's worship and bow down.
   Let's kneel in front of the LORD, our maker,
      because he is our God
         and we are the people in his care,
            the flock that he leads.
If only you would listen to him today!

Psalm 95:6–7

If indeed you call out for insight,
if you ask aloud for understanding,
if you search for wisdom as if it were money
   and hunt for it as if it were hidden treasure,
then you will understand the fear of the LORD
   and you will find the knowledge of God.

Proverbs 2:3–5

Guard your heart more than anything else,
   because the source of your life flows from it.

Proverbs 4:23

The person who is greatest among you will be your servant. Whoever honors himself will be humbled, and whoever humbles himself will be honored.

Matthew 23:11–12

I, a prisoner in the Lord, encourage you to live the kind of life which proves that God has called you. Be humble and gentle in every way. Be patient with each other and lovingly accept each other. Through the peace that ties you together, do your best to maintain the unity that the Spirit gives.

Ephesians 4:1–3

You were taught to change the way you were living. The person you used to be will ruin you through desires that deceive you. However, you were taught to have a new attitude. You were also taught to become a new person created to be like God, truly righteous and holy.

Ephesians 4:22–24

However, the person who continues to study God's perfect laws that make people free and who remains committed to them will be blessed. People like that don't merely listen and forget; they actually do what God's laws say.

James 1:25

Furthermore, all of you must serve each other with humility, because God opposes the arrogant but favors the humble. Be humbled by God's power so that when the right time comes he will honor you.

1 Peter 5:5–6

Communication

The mouth of the righteous person reflects on
    wisdom.
    His tongue speaks what is fair.
The teachings of his God are in his heart.
    His feet do not slip.

                            Psalm 37:30–31

A person's anxiety will weigh him down,
    but an encouraging word makes him joyful.

                            Proverbs 12:25

A gentle answer turns away rage,
    but a harsh word stirs up anger.
The tongues of wise people give good expression to
    knowledge,
    but the mouths of fools pour out a flood of
        stupidity.

                            Proverbs 15:1–2

A soothing tongue is a tree of life,
    but a deceitful tongue breaks the spirit.

                            Proverbs 15:4

A wise person's heart controls his speech,
   and what he says helps others learn.
Pleasant words are like honey from a honeycomb—
   sweet to the spirit and healthy for the body.

Proverbs 16:23–24

Whoever guards his mouth and his tongue keeps
   himself out of trouble.

Proverbs 21:23

Like golden apples in silver settings,
   so is a word spoken at the right time.

Proverbs 25:11

Instead, as we lovingly speak the truth, we will grow up completely in our relationship to Christ, who is the head.

Ephesians 4:15

Don't say anything that would hurt another person. Instead, speak only what is good so that you can give help wherever it is needed. That way, what you say will help those who hear you.

Ephesians 4:29

Everything you say should be kind and well thought out so that you know how to answer everyone.

Colossians 4:6

So admit your sins to each other, and pray for each other so that you will be healed.

James 5:16

People who want to live a full life and enjoy good
  days
    must keep their tongues from saying evil things,
    and their lips from speaking deceitful things.

1 Peter 3:10

Whoever speaks must speak God's words. Whoever serves must serve with the strength God supplies so that in every way God receives glory through Jesus Christ. Glory and power belong to Jesus Christ forever and ever! Amen.

1 Peter 4:11

Gentleness

But the spiritual nature produces love, joy, peace, patience, kindness, goodness, faithfulness, gentleness, and self-control. There are no laws against things like that.

Galatians 5:22–23

Be humble and gentle in every way. Be patient with each other and lovingly accept each other.

Ephesians 4:2

Let everyone know how considerate you are. The Lord is near.

Philippians 4:5

Rather, beauty is something internal that can't be destroyed. Beauty expresses itself in a gentle and quiet attitude which God considers precious.

1 Peter 3:4

Don't pay people back with evil for the evil they do to you, or ridicule those who ridicule you. Instead, bless them, because you were called to inherit a blessing.

1 Peter 3:9

But dedicate your lives to Christ as Lord. Always be ready to defend your confidence in God when anyone asks you to explain it. However, make your defense with gentleness and respect. Keep your conscience clear. Then those who treat the good Christian life you live with contempt will feel ashamed that they have ridiculed you.

1 Peter 3:15–16

Goals

A person's steps are directed by the LORD,
and the LORD delights in his way.

Psalm 37:23

But first, be concerned about his kingdom and what has his approval. Then all these things will be provided for you.

Matthew 6:33

Don't you realize that everyone who runs in a race runs to win, but only one runner gets the prize? Run like them, so that you can win.

1 Corinthians 9:24

In the same way, since you're eager to have spiritual gifts, try to excel in them so that you help the church grow.

1 Corinthians 14:12

Whether we live in the body or move out of it, our goal is to be pleasing to him.

2 Corinthians 5:9

Brothers and sisters, I can't consider myself a winner yet. This is what I do: I don't look back, I lengthen my stride, and I run straight toward the goal to win the prize that God's heavenly call offers in Christ Jesus.

Philippians 3:13–14

Humility

He leads humble people to do what is right,
and he teaches them his way.

Psalm 25:9

The LORD is near to those whose hearts are humble.
He saves those whose spirits are crushed.

Psalm 34:18

The High and Lofty One lives forever, and his name
is holy.
This is what he says:
I live in a high and holy place.
But I am with those who are crushed and humble.
I will renew the spirit of those who are humble
and the courage of those who are crushed.

Isaiah 57:15

I, a prisoner in the Lord, encourage you to live the kind
of life which proves that God has called you. Be humble and
gentle in every way. Be patient with each other and lovingly
accept each other. Through the peace that ties you together,
do your best to maintain the unity that the Spirit gives.

Ephesians 4:1–3

As holy people whom God has chosen and loved, be sympathetic, kind, humble, gentle, and patient. Put up with each other, and forgive each other if anyone has a complaint. Forgive as the Lord forgave you. Above all, be loving. This ties everything together perfectly. Also, let Christ's peace control you. God has called you into this peace by bringing you into one body. Be thankful.

Colossians 3:12–15

Humble yourselves in the Lord's presence. Then he will give you a high position.

James 4:10

Finally, everyone must live in harmony, be sympathetic, love each other, have compassion, and be humble. Don't pay people back with evil for the evil they do to you, or ridicule those who ridicule you. Instead, bless them, because you were called to inherit a blessing.

1 Peter 3:8–9

Young people, in a similar way, place yourselves under the authority of spiritual leaders. Furthermore, all of you must serve each other with humility, because God opposes the arrogant but favors the humble. Be humbled by God's power so that when the right time comes he will honor you.

1 Peter 5:5–6

Knowledge

Gullible people are gifted with stupidity,
> but sensible people are crowned with knowledge.

Proverbs 14:18

God gives wisdom, knowledge, and joy to anyone who pleases him.

Ecclesiastes 2:26

We are his servants because the same God who said that light should shine out of darkness has given us light. For that reason we bring to light the knowledge about God's glory which shines from Christ's face.

2 Corinthians 4:6

Then you will have deeper insight. You will know the confidence that he calls you to have and the glorious wealth that God's people will inherit. You will also know the unlimited greatness of his power as it works with might and strength for us, the believers.

Ephesians 1:18–19

I pray that your love will keep on growing because of your knowledge and insight. That way you will be able to determine what is best and be pure and blameless until the day of Christ.

Philippians 1:9–10

For this reason we have not stopped praying for you since the day we heard about you. We ask God to fill you with the knowledge of his will through every kind of spiritual wisdom and insight.

Colossians 1:9

I've written this to those who believe in the Son of God so that they will know that they have eternal life.

1 John 5:13

Obedience to Him

I will give you a new heart and put a new spirit in you. I will remove your stubborn hearts and give you obedient hearts. I will put my Spirit in you. I will enable you to live by my laws, and you will obey my rules.

Ezekiel 36:26–27

Therefore, everyone who hears what I say and obeys it will be like a wise person who built a house on rock. Rain poured, and floods came. Winds blew and beat against that house. But it did not collapse, because its foundation was on rock.

Matthew 7:24–25

Jesus replied, "Rather, how blessed are those who hear and obey God's word."

Luke 11:28

Whoever knows and obeys my commandments is the person who loves me. Those who love me will have my Father's love, and I, too, will love them and show myself to them.

John 14:21

Jesus answered him, "Those who love me will do what I say. My Father will love them, and we will go to them and make our home with them."

John 14:23

I have loved you the same way the Father has loved me. So live in my love. If you obey my commandments, you will live in my love. I have obeyed my Father's commandments, and in that way I live in his love. I have told you this so that you will be as joyful as I am, and your joy will be complete. Love each other as I have loved you. This is what I'm commanding you to do. The greatest love you can show is to give your life for your friends.

John 15:9–13

In the same way, brothers and sisters, you have died to the laws in Moses' Teachings through Christ's body. You belong to someone else, the one who was brought back to life.

As a result, we can do what God wants. While we were living under the influence of our corrupt nature, sinful passions were at work throughout our bodies. Stirred up by the laws in Moses' Teachings, our sinful passions did things that result in death.

Romans 7:4–5

My dear friends, you have always obeyed, not only when I was with you but even more now that I'm absent. In the same way continue to work out your salvation with fear and trembling. It is God who produces in you the desires and actions that please him.

Philippians 2:12–13

On earth we have fathers who disciplined us, and we respect them. Shouldn't we place ourselves under the authority of God, the father of spirits, so that we will live? For a short time our fathers disciplined us as they thought best. Yet, God disciplines us for our own good so that we can become holy like him.

Hebrews 12:9–10

However, the person who continues to study God's perfect laws that make people free and who remains committed to them will be blessed. People like that don't merely listen and forget; they actually do what God's laws say.

James 1:25

But whoever obeys what Christ says is the kind of person in whom God's love is perfected. That's how we know we are in Christ.

1 John 2:5

Patience and Perseverance

I waited patiently for the LORD.
He turned to me and heard my cry for help.
He pulled me out of a horrible pit,
out of the mud and clay.
He set my feet on a rock
and made my steps secure.
He placed a new song in my mouth,
a song of praise to our God.
Many will see this and worship.
They will trust the LORD.

Psalm 40:1–3

But that's not all. We also brag when we are suffering. We know that suffering creates endurance, endurance creates character, and character creates confidence.

Romans 5:3–4

We can't allow ourselves to get tired of living the right way. Certainly, each of us will receive everlasting life at the proper time, if we don't give up.

Galatians 6:9

You know that such testing of your faith produces endurance. Endure until your testing is over. Then you will be mature and complete, and you won't need anything.

James 1:3–4

Blessed are those who endure when they are tested. When they pass the test, they will receive the crown of life that God has promised to those who love him.

James 1:12

Brothers and sisters, be patient until the Lord comes again. See how farmers wait for their precious crops to grow. They wait patiently for fall and spring rains. You, too, must be patient. Don't give up hope. The Lord will soon be here.

James 5:7–8

God, who shows you his kindness and who has called you through Christ Jesus to his eternal glory, will restore you, strengthen you, make you strong, and support you as you suffer for a little while.

1 Peter 5:10

Proper Ambition

He will give you your heart's desire
and carry out all your plans.

Psalm 20:4

Be happy with the Lord,
and he will give you the desires of your heart.

Psalm 37:4

A lazy person craves food and there is none,
but the appetite of hard-working people is
satisfied.

Proverbs 13:4

A person may plan his own journey,
but the Lord directs his steps.

Proverbs 16:9

Many plans are in the human heart,
but the advice of the Lord will endure.

Proverbs 19:21

Whoever wants to be most important among you will be your slave. It's the same way with the Son of Man. He didn't come so that others could serve him. He came to serve and to give his life as a ransom for many people.

Matthew 20:27–28

I'm convinced that God, who began this good work in you, will carry it through to completion on the day of Christ Jesus.

Philippians 1:6

Each of you as a good manager must use the gift that God has given you to serve others. Whoever speaks must speak God's words. Whoever serves must serve with the strength God supplies so that in every way God receives glory through Jesus Christ. Glory and power belong to Jesus Christ forever and ever! Amen.

1 Peter 4:10–11

Proper Self-Esteem

Realize that the LORD alone is God.
  He made us, and we are his.
  We are his people and the sheep in his care.

Psalm 100:3

O LORD, you have examined me, and you know me.
  You alone know when I sit down and when I get
    up.
  You read my thoughts from far away.
  You watch me when I travel and when I rest.
  You are familiar with all my ways.
    Even before there is a single word on my
      tongue,
      you know all about it, LORD.
  You are all around me—in front of me and in
    back of me.
  You lay your hand on me.
    Such knowledge is beyond my grasp.
    It is so high I cannot reach it.

Psalm 139:1–6

You alone created my inner being.
You knitted me together inside my mother.
I will give thanks to you
    because I have been so amazingly and miracu-
        lously made.
        Your works are miraculous, and my soul is
            fully aware of this.

Psalm 139:13–14

But now, LORD, you are our Father.
    We are the clay, and you are our potter.
    We are the work of your hands.

Isaiah 64:8

Aren't two sparrows sold for a penny? Not one of them will fall to the ground without your Father's permission. Every hair on your head has been counted.

Matthew 10:29–30

Don't you know that you are God's temple and that God's Spirit lives in you?

1 Corinthians 3:16

Before the creation of the world, he chose us through Christ to be holy and perfect in his presence. Because of his love he had already decided to adopt us through Jesus Christ. He freely chose to do this.

Ephesians 1:4–5

And you've become a new person. This new person is continually renewed in knowledge to be like its Creator.

Colossians 3:10

Relationships

Whoever walks with wise people will be wise,
  but whoever associates with fools will suffer.

Proverbs 13:20

Friends can destroy one another,
  but a loving friend can stick closer than family.

Proverbs 18:24

I'm giving you a new commandment: Love each other in the same way that I have loved you. Everyone will know that you are my disciples because of your love for each other.

John 13:34–35

Love each other as I have loved you. This is what I'm commanding you to do. The greatest love you can show is to give your life for your friends.

John 15:12–13

Be devoted to each other like a loving family. Excel in showing respect for each other.

Romans 12:10

Be happy with those who are happy. Be sad with those who are sad. Live in harmony with each other. Don't be arrogant, but be friendly to humble people. Don't think that you are smarter than you really are.

Romans 12:15–16

The body is one unit and yet has many parts. As all the parts form one body, so it is with Christ.

1 Corinthians 12:12

You were indeed called to be free, brothers and sisters. Don't turn this freedom into an excuse for your corrupt nature to express itself. Rather, serve each other through love.

Galatians 5:13

Help carry each other's burdens. In this way you will follow Christ's teachings.

Galatians 6:2

We must also consider how to encourage each other to show love and to do good things. We should not stop gathering together with other believers, as some of you are doing. Instead, we must continue to encourage each other even more as we see the day of the Lord coming.

Hebrews 10:24–25

Continue to love each other. Don't forget to show hospitality to believers you don't know. By doing this some believers have shown hospitality to angels without being aware of it.

Hebrews 13:1–2

But if we live in the light in the same way that God is in the light, we have a relationship with each other. And the blood of his Son Jesus cleanses us from every sin.

1 John 1:7

Seeking Him

Search for the LORD and his strength.
Always seek his presence.
Remember the miracles he performed,
   the amazing things he did and the judgments he
      pronounced.

1 Chronicles 16:11–12

I went to the LORD for help.
   He answered me and rescued me from all my
      fears.
All who look to him will be radiant.
   Their faces will never be covered with shame.

Psalm 34:4–5

O God, you are my God.
   At dawn I search for you.
      My soul thirsts for you.
      My body longs for you
         in a dry, parched land where there is no
            water.
So I look for you in the holy place
   to see your power and your glory.

Psalm 63:1–2

God wanted his people throughout the world to know the glorious riches of this mystery—which is Christ living in you, giving you the hope of glory.

Colossians 1:27

Every Scripture passage is inspired by God. All of them are useful for teaching, pointing out errors, correcting people, and training them for a life that has God's approval. They equip God's servants so that they are completely prepared to do good things.

2 Timothy 3:16–17

In the past God spoke to our ancestors at many different times and in many different ways through the prophets. In these last days he has spoken to us through his Son. God made his Son responsible for everything. His Son is the one through whom God made the universe.

Hebrews 1:1–2

Come close to God, and he will come close to you. Clean up your lives, you sinners, and clear your minds, you doubters.

James 4:8

Thought Life

Trust the LORD with all your heart,
   and do not rely on your own understanding.
In all your ways acknowledge him,
   and he will make your paths smooth.
Do not consider yourself wise.
Fear the LORD, and turn away from evil.

Proverbs 3:5–7

At the same time the Spirit also helps us in our weakness, because we don't know how to pray for what we need. But the Spirit intercedes along with our groans that cannot be expressed in words. The one who searches our hearts knows what the Spirit has in mind. The Spirit intercedes for God's people the way God wants him to.

Romans 8:26–27

Through the blood of his Son, we are set free from our sins. God forgives our failures because of his overflowing kindness. He poured out his kindness by giving us every kind of wisdom and insight when he revealed the mystery of his plan to us. He had decided to do this through Christ.

Ephesians 1:7–9

God didn't give us a cowardly spirit but a spirit of power, love, and good judgment.

2 Timothy 1:7

If any of you needs wisdom to know what you should do, you should ask God, and he will give it to you. God is generous to everyone and doesn't find fault with them.

James 1:5

The end of everything is near. Therefore, practice self-control, and keep your minds clear so that you can pray.

1 Peter 4:7

Trust

Those who know your name trust you, O Lord,
  because you have never deserted those who seek
    your help.

Psalm 9:10

You have seen it; yes, you have taken note of trouble
    and grief
  and placed them under your control.
    The victim entrusts himself to you.
You alone have been the helper of orphans.

Psalm 10:14

Some rely on chariots and others on horses,
  but we will boast in the name of the Lord our
    God.
    They will sink to their knees and fall,
      but we will rise and stand firm.

Psalm 20:7–8

We wait for the Lord.
  He is our help and our shield.
  In him our hearts find joy.
  In his holy name we trust.

Psalm 33:20–21

Whoever lives under the shelter of the Most High
     will remain in the shadow of the Almighty.
I will say to the LORD,
     "You are my refuge and my fortress, my God in
          whom I trust."

                                        Psalm 91:1–2

Whoever gives attention to the LORD's word
          prospers,
     and blessed is the person who trusts the LORD.

                                        Proverbs 16:20

A person's fear sets a trap for him,
     but one who trusts the LORD is safe.

                                        Proverbs 29:25

Trust the LORD always,
     because the LORD, the LORD alone, is an everlast-
          ing rock.

                                        Isaiah 26:4

Blessed is the person who trusts the LORD.
     The LORD will be his confidence.
He will be like a tree that is planted by water.
     It will send its roots down to a stream.
     It will not be afraid in the heat of summer.
          Its leaves will turn green.
     It will not be anxious during droughts.
          It will not stop producing fruit.

                                        Jeremiah 17:7–8

Understanding
and Wisdom

The fear of the LORD is the beginning of wisdom.
Good sense is shown by everyone who follows God's
  guiding principles.
His praise continues forever.

Psalm 111:10

From your guiding principles I gain understanding.
 That is why I hate every path that leads to lying.

Psalm 119:104

The LORD gives wisdom.
 From his mouth come knowledge and
  understanding.
  He has reserved priceless wisdom for decent
   people.
He is a shield for those who walk in integrity
 in order to guard those on paths of justice
  and to watch over the way of his godly ones.

Proverbs 2:6–8

Blessed is the one who finds wisdom
   and the one who obtains understanding.
      The profit gained from wisdom is greater than
         the profit gained from silver.
            Its yield is better than fine gold.

Proverbs 3:13–14

The beginning of wisdom is to acquire wisdom.
Acquire understanding with all that you have.
Cherish wisdom.
   It will raise you up.
   It will bring you honor when you embrace it.
   It will give you a graceful garland for your head.
   It will hand you a beautiful crown.

Proverbs 4:7–9

I have taught you the way of wisdom.
I have guided you along decent paths.
   When you walk, your stride will not be hampered.
   Even if you run, you will not stumble.

Proverbs 4:11–12

The knowledge of wisdom is like that for your soul.
   If you find it, then there is a future,
      and your hope will never be cut off.

Proverbs 24:14

Then a shoot will come out from the stump of Jesse,
   and a branch from its roots will bear fruit.
The Spirit of the Lord will rest on him—
   the Spirit of wisdom and understanding,

the Spirit of advice and power,
the Spirit of knowledge and fear of the LORD.

Isaiah 11:1–2

Through the blood of his Son, we are set free from our sins. God forgives our failures because of his overflowing kindness. He poured out his kindness by giving us every kind of wisdom and insight when he revealed the mystery of his plan to us. He had decided to do this through Christ.

Ephesians 1:7–9

Because they are united in love, I work so that they may be encouraged by all the riches that come from a complete understanding of Christ. He is the mystery of God. God has hidden all the treasures of wisdom and knowledge in Christ.

Colossians 2:2–3

If any of you needs wisdom to know what you should do, you should ask God, and he will give it to you. God is generous to everyone and doesn't find fault with them.

James 1:5

Do any of you have wisdom and insight? Show this by living the right way with the humility that comes from wisdom.

James 3:13

However, the wisdom that comes from above is first of all pure. Then it is peaceful, gentle, obedient, filled with mercy and good deeds, impartial, and sincere.

James 3:17

Unity

See how good and pleasant it is
   when brothers and sisters live together in
      harmony!

Psalm 133:1

I have given them the glory that you gave me. I did this so that they are united in the same way we are. I am in them, and you are in me. So they are completely united. In this way the world knows that you have sent me and that you have loved them in the same way you have loved me.

John 17:22–23

May God, who gives you this endurance and encouragement, allow you to live in harmony with each other by following the example of Christ Jesus.

Romans 15:5

By one Spirit we were all baptized into one body. Whether we are Jewish or Greek, slave or free, God gave all of us one Spirit to drink.

1 Corinthians 12:13

There are neither Jews nor Greeks, slaves nor free people, males nor females. You are all the same in Christ Jesus.

Galatians 3:28

Through the peace that ties you together, do your best to maintain the unity that the Spirit gives. There is one body and one Spirit. In the same way you were called to share one hope. There is one Lord, one faith, one baptism, one God and Father of all, who is over everything, through everything, and in everything.

Ephesians 4:3–6

He makes the whole body fit together and unites it through the support of every joint. As each and every part does its job, he makes the body grow so that it builds itself up in love.

Ephesians 4:16

Christ makes the whole body grow as God wants it to, through support and unity given by the joints and ligaments.

Colossians 2:19

However, you are chosen people, a royal priesthood, a holy nation, people who belong to God. You were chosen to tell about the excellent qualities of God, who called you out of darkness into his marvelous light.

1 Peter 2:9

Finally, everyone must live in harmony, be sympathetic, love each other, have compassion, and be humble.

1 Peter 3:8

God Promises to Help
Grow Women of . . .

Accomplishment

With you I can attack a line of soldiers.
With my God I can break through barricades.

Psalm 18:29

Blessed are those who find strength in you.
    Their hearts are on the road that leads to you.
        As they pass through a valley where balsam
            trees grow,
        they make it a place of springs.
            The early rains cover it with blessings.
                Their strength grows as they go along
                until each one of them appears
                in front of God in Zion.

Psalm 84:5–7

Entrust your efforts to the LORD,
    and your plans will succeed.

Proverbs 16:3

Those who serve me must follow me. My servants will be with me wherever I will be. If people serve me, the Father will honor them.

John 12:26

We can't allow ourselves to get tired of living the right way. Certainly, each of us will receive everlasting life at the proper time, if we don't give up.

Galatians 6:9

These things that I once considered valuable, I now consider worthless for Christ. It's far more than that! I consider everything else worthless because I'm much better off knowing Christ Jesus my Lord. It's because of him that I think of everything as worthless. I threw it all away in order to gain Christ and to have a relationship with him. This means that I didn't receive God's approval by obeying his laws. The opposite is true! I have God's approval through faith in Christ. This is the approval that comes from God and is based on faith.

Philippians 3:7–9

I have fought the good fight. I have completed the race. I have kept the faith. The prize that shows I have God's approval is now waiting for me. The Lord, who is a fair judge, will give me that prize on that day. He will give it not only to me but also to everyone who is eagerly waiting for him to come again.

2 Timothy 4:7–8

Character

Yet, the righteous person clings to his way,
    and the one with clean hands grows stronger.

Job 17:9

The Lord is righteous.
    He loves a righteous way of life.
        Decent people will see his face.

Psalm 11:7

        Light will shine in the dark for a decent
        person.
            He is merciful, compassionate, and fair.
All goes well for the person who is generous and
    lends willingly.
    He earns an honest living.
        He will never fail.
        A righteous person will always be remembered.

Psalm 112:4–6

The highway of decent people turns away from evil.
Whoever watches his way preserves his own life.

Proverbs 16:17

Charm is deceptive, and beauty evaporates,
>   but a woman who has the fear of the LORD should
>   be praised.
Reward her for what she has done,
>   and let her achievements praise her at the city
>   gates.

Proverbs 31:30–31

We also brag when we are suffering. We know that suffering creates endurance, endurance creates character, and character creates confidence. We're not ashamed to have this confidence, because God's love has been poured into our hearts by the Holy Spirit, who has been given to us.

Romans 5:3–5

Training the body helps a little, but godly living helps in every way. Godly living has the promise of life now and in the world to come.

1 Timothy 4:8

Make every effort to add integrity to your faith; and to integrity add knowledge; to knowledge add self-control; to self-control add endurance; to endurance add godliness; to godliness add Christian affection; and to Christian affection add love. If you have these qualities and they are increasing, it demonstrates that your knowledge about our Lord Jesus Christ is living and productive. If these qualities aren't present in your life, you're shortsighted and have forgotten that you were cleansed from your past sins.

2 Peter 1:5–9

Commitment

The LORD's eyes scan the whole world to find those whose hearts are committed to him and to strengthen them.

2 Chronicles 16:9

But from everlasting to everlasting,
   the LORD's mercy is on those who fear him.
   His righteousness belongs
      to their children and grandchildren,
      to those who are faithful to his promise,
      to those who remember to follow his guiding
         principles.

Psalm 103:17–18

Jesus said to them, "I can guarantee this truth: Anyone who gave up his home, wife, brothers, parents, or children because of the kingdom of God will certainly receive many times as much in this life and will receive eternal life in the world to come."

Luke 18:29–30

Those who serve me must follow me. My servants will be with me wherever I will be. If people serve me, the Father will honor them.

John 12:26

For this reason I suffer as I do. However, I'm not ashamed. I know whom I trust. I'm convinced that he is able to protect what he had entrusted to me until that day.

2 Timothy 1:12

Do your best to present yourself to God as a tried-and-true worker who isn't ashamed to teach the word of truth correctly.

2 Timothy 2:15

But dedicate your lives to Christ as Lord. Always be ready to defend your confidence in God when anyone asks you to explain it. However, make your defense with gentleness and respect.

1 Peter 3:15

Those who suffer because that is God's will for them must entrust themselves to a faithful creator and continue to do what is good.

1 Peter 4:19

Now, dear children, live in Christ. Then, when he appears we will have confidence, and when he comes we won't turn from him in shame.

1 John 2:28

Dear friends, use your most holy faith to grow. Pray with the Holy Spirit's help. Remain in God's love as you look for the mercy of our Lord Jesus Christ to give you eternal life.

Jude 20–21

I am coming soon! Hold on to what you have so that no one takes your crown.

I will make everyone who wins the victory a pillar in the temple of my God. They will never leave it again. I will write on them the name of my God, the name of the city of my God (the New Jerusalem coming down out of heaven from my God), and my new name.

Revelation 3:11–12

Confidence

I always keep the LORD in front of me.
>   When he is by my side, I cannot be moved.
>>   That is why my heart is glad and my soul
>>>   rejoices.
>>   My body rests securely.

Psalm 16:8–9

The LORD is my light and my salvation.
>   Who is there to fear?

The LORD is my life's fortress.
>   Who is there to be afraid of?

Evildoers closed in on me to tear me to pieces.
>   My opponents and enemies stumbled and fell.
>>   Even though an army sets up camp against me,
>>   my heart will not be afraid.
>>   Even though a war breaks out against me,
>>   I will still have confidence in the LORD.

Psalm 27:1–3

You, O LORD, are my refuge!
You have made the Most High your home.
    No harm will come to you.
    No sickness will come near your house.
He will put his angels in charge of you
    to protect you in all your ways.
        They will carry you in their hands
            so that you never hit your foot against a
                rock.
        You will step on lions and cobras.
        You will trample young lions and snakes.

Psalm 91:9–13

Do not be afraid of sudden terror
    or of the destruction of wicked people when it
        comes.
    The LORD will be your confidence.
    He will keep your foot from getting caught.

Proverbs 3:25–26

Blessed is the person who trusts the LORD.
    The LORD will be his confidence.

Jeremiah 17:7

We can go to God with bold confidence through faith
in Christ.

Ephesians 3:12

Every time I pray for all of you, I do it with joy. I can do this because of the partnership we've had with you in the Good News from the first day you believed until now. I'm convinced that God, who began this good work in you, will carry it through to completion on the day of Christ Jesus.

Philippians 1:4–6

So we can go confidently to the throne of God's kindness to receive mercy and find kindness, which will help us at the right time.

Hebrews 4:16

We have this confidence as a sure and strong anchor for our lives. This confidence goes into the holy place behind the curtain where Jesus went before us on our behalf. He has become the chief priest forever in the way Melchizedek was a priest.

Hebrews 6:19–20

Brothers and sisters, because of the blood of Jesus we can now confidently go into the holy place. Jesus has opened a new and living way for us to go through the curtain. (The curtain is his own body.) We have a superior priest in charge of God's house. We have been sprinkled with his blood to free us from a guilty conscience, and our bodies have been washed with clean water. So we must continue to come to him with a sincere heart and strong faith.

Hebrews 10:19–22

So don't lose your confidence. It will bring you a great reward. You need endurance so that after you have done what God wants you to do, you can receive what he has promised.

Hebrews 10:35–36

Dear friends, if our conscience doesn't condemn us, we can boldly look to God and receive from him anything we ask. We receive it because we obey his commandments and do what pleases him. This is his commandment: to believe in his Son, the one named Jesus Christ, and to love each other as he commanded us.

1 John 3:21–23

We are confident that God listens to us if we ask for anything that has his approval. We know that he listens to our requests. So we know that we already have what we ask him for.

1 John 5:14–15

Contentment

The LORD is my shepherd.
I am never in need.

Psalm 23:1

Better a few possessions gained honestly
than many gained through injustice.

Proverbs 16:8

The fear of the LORD leads to life,
and such a person will rest easy without suffering
harm.

Proverbs 19:23

So I tell you to stop worrying about what you will eat,
drink, or wear. Isn't life more than food and the body more
than clothes?

Look at the birds. They don't plant, harvest, or gather
the harvest into barns. Yet, your heavenly Father feeds them.
Aren't you worth more than they?

Matthew 6:25–26

Everyone should live the life that the Lord gave him when God called him. This is the guideline I use in every church.

1 Corinthians 7:17

A godly life brings huge profits to people who are content with what they have. We didn't bring anything into the world, and we can't take anything out of it. As long as we have food and clothes, we should be satisfied.

1 Timothy 6:6–8

Don't love money. Be happy with what you have because God has said, "I will never abandon you or leave you."

Hebrews 13:5

Courage

Even though I walk through the dark valley of
    death,
  because you are with me, I fear no harm.
    Your rod and your staff give me courage.

Psalm 23:4

·The Lord is my light and my salvation.
    Who is there to fear?
The Lord is my life's fortress.
    Who is there to be afraid of?

Psalm 27:1

Be strong, all who wait with hope for the Lord,
    and let your heart be courageous.

Psalm 31:24

Do not be afraid of sudden terror
    or of the destruction of wicked people when it
        comes.
    The Lord will be your confidence.
    He will keep your foot from getting caught.

Proverbs 3:25–26

Don't be afraid, because I am with you.
Don't be intimidated; I am your God.
  I will strengthen you.
  I will help you.
  I will support you with my victorious right hand.

Isaiah 41:10

The High and Lofty One lives forever, and his name
  is holy.
This is what he says:
I live in a high and holy place.
  But I am with those who are crushed and humble.
    I will renew the spirit of those who are humble
      and the courage of those who are crushed.

Isaiah 57:15

I eagerly expect and hope that I will have nothing to
be ashamed of. I will speak very boldly and honor Christ
in my body, now as always, whether I live or die. Christ
means everything to me in this life, and when I die I'll
have even more.

Philippians 1:20–21

But Christ is a faithful son in charge of God's household.
We are his household if we continue to have courage and
to be proud of the confidence we have.

Hebrews 3:6

No fear exists where his love is. Rather, perfect love gets
rid of fear, because fear involves punishment. The person
who lives in fear doesn't have perfect love.

1 John 4:18

Determination

The Almighty Lᴏʀᴅ helps me.
That is why I will not be ashamed.
I have set my face like a flint.
I know that I will not be put to shame.

Isaiah 50:7

So, then, brothers and sisters, don't let anyone move you off the foundation of your faith. Always excel in the work you do for the Lord. You know that the hard work you do for the Lord is not pointless.

1 Corinthians 15:58

We can't allow ourselves to get tired of living the right way. Certainly, each of us will receive everlasting life at the proper time, if we don't give up.

Galatians 6:9

Finally, receive your power from the Lord and from his mighty strength. Put on all the armor that God supplies. In this way you can take a stand against the devil's strategies. This is not a wrestling match against a human opponent. We are wrestling with rulers, authorities, the powers who govern this world of darkness, and spiritual forces that control evil in the heavenly world. For this reason, take up all the armor that God supplies. Then you will be able to take a stand during these evil days. Once you have overcome all obstacles, you will be able to stand your ground.

Ephesians 6:10–13

I am coming soon! Hold on to what you have so that no one takes your crown.

Revelation 3:11

Faith

You saved me from death.
You saved my eyes from tears and my feet from
    stumbling.
I will walk in the LORD's presence in this world of
    the living.
I kept my faith even when I said,
  "I am suffering terribly."
I also said when I was panic-stricken,
  "Everyone is undependable."
How can I repay the LORD
  for all the good that he has done for me?

Psalm 116:8–12

He told them, "Because you have so little faith. I can
guarantee this truth: If your faith is the size of a mustard
seed, you can say to this mountain, 'Move from here to
there,' and it will move. Nothing will be impossible for
you."

Matthew 17:20

I can guarantee this truth: Those who believe in me will
do the things that I am doing. They will do even greater
things because I am going to the Father.

John 14:12

God's approval is revealed in this Good News. This approval begins and ends with faith as Scripture says, "The person who has God's approval will live by faith."

Romans 1:17

Now that we have God's approval by faith, we have peace with God because of what our Lord Jesus Christ has done. Through Christ we can approach God and stand in his favor. So we brag because of our confidence that we will receive glory from God.

Romans 5:1–2

God saved you through faith as an act of kindness. You had nothing to do with it. Being saved is a gift from God. It's not the result of anything you've done, so no one can brag about it.

Ephesians 2:8–9

Through him you believe in God who brought Christ back to life and gave him glory. So your faith and confidence are in God.

1 Peter 1:21

Who wins the victory over the world? Isn't it the person who believes that Jesus is the Son of God?

1 John 5:5

Dear friends, use your most holy faith to grow. Pray with the Holy Spirit's help. Remain in God's love as you look for the mercy of our Lord Jesus Christ to give you eternal life.

Jude 20–21

Faithfulness

In dealing with faithful people you are faithful,
  with innocent warriors you are innocent.

                    2 Samuel 22:26

Love the LORD, all you godly ones!
  The LORD protects faithful people,
    but he pays back in full those who act
      arrogantly.

                    Psalm 31:23

My eyes will be watching the faithful people in the
    land
  so that they may live with me.
    The person who lives with integrity will serve
      me.
The one who does deceitful things will not stay in
    my home.
The one who tells lies will not remain in my
    presence.

                    Psalm 101:6–7

  I will give you a new heart and put a new spirit in you.
I will remove your stubborn hearts and give you obedient

hearts. I will put my Spirit in you. I will enable you to live by my laws, and you will obey my rules.

Ezekiel 36:26–27

Whoever can be trusted with very little can also be trusted with a lot. Whoever is dishonest with very little is dishonest with a lot. Therefore, if you can't be trusted with wealth that is often used dishonestly, who will trust you with wealth that is real? If you can't be trusted with someone else's wealth, who will give you your own?

A servant cannot serve two masters. He will hate the first master and love the second, or he will be devoted to the first and despise the second. You cannot serve God and wealth.

Luke 16:10–13

But the spiritual nature produces love, joy, peace, patience, kindness, goodness, faithfulness, gentleness, and self-control. There are no laws against things like that.

Galatians 5:22–23

Whatever you do, do it wholeheartedly as though you were working for your real master and not merely for humans. You know that your real master will give you an inheritance as your reward. It is Christ, your real master, whom you are serving. The person who does wrong will be paid back for the wrong he has done. God does not play favorites.

Colossians 3:23–25

Don't be afraid of what you are going to suffer. The devil is going to throw some of you into prison so that you may be tested. Your suffering will go on for ten days. Be faithful until death, and I will give you the crown of life.

Revelation 2:10

Freedom

You will know the truth, and the truth will set you free.

John 8:32

So if the Son sets you free, you will be absolutely free.

John 8:36

We know that the person we used to be was crucified with him to put an end to sin in our bodies. Because of this we are no longer slaves to sin. The person who has died has been freed from sin.

Romans 6:6–7

Now you have been freed from sin and have become God's slaves. This results in a holy life and, finally, in everlasting life.

Romans 6:22

This Lord is the Spirit. Wherever the Lord's Spirit is, there is freedom.

2 Corinthians 3:17

Christ has freed us so that we may enjoy the benefits of freedom. Therefore, be firm in this freedom, and don't become slaves again.

Galatians 5:1

You were indeed called to be free, brothers and sisters. Don't turn this freedom into an excuse for your corrupt nature to express itself. Rather, serve each other through love.

Galatians 5:13

Live as free people, but don't hide behind your freedom when you do evil. Instead, use your freedom to serve God.

1 Peter 2:16

Generosity

I have been young, and now I am old,
  but I have never seen a righteous person
      abandoned
  or his descendants begging for food.
      He is always generous and lends freely.
      His descendants are a blessing.

Psalm 37:25–26

All goes well for the person who is generous and
    lends willingly.
  He earns an honest living.

Psalm 112:5

A generous person will be made rich,
  and whoever satisfies others will himself be
      satisfied.

Proverbs 11:25

Whoever is generous will be blessed
  because he has shared his food with the poor.

Proverbs 22:9

Whoever gives to the poor lacks nothing.
Whoever ignores the poor receives many curses.

Proverbs 28:27

I can guarantee this truth: Whoever gives any of my humble followers a cup of cold water because that person is my disciple will certainly never lose his reward.

Matthew 10:42

Give, and you will receive. A large quantity, pressed together, shaken down, and running over will be put into your pocket. The standards you use for others will be applied to you.

Luke 6:38

God in his kindness gave each of us different gifts. If your gift is speaking what God has revealed, make sure what you say agrees with the Christian faith. If your gift is serving, then devote yourself to serving. If it is teaching, devote yourself to teaching. If it is encouraging others, devote yourself to giving encouragement. If it is sharing, be generous. If it is leadership, lead enthusiastically. If it is helping people in need, help them cheerfully.

Romans 12:6–8

Remember this: The farmer who plants a few seeds will have a very small harvest. But the farmer who plants because he has received God's blessings will receive a harvest of God's blessings in return.

2 Corinthians 9:6

Tell them to do good, to do a lot of good things, to be generous, and to share. By doing this they store up a treasure for themselves which is a good foundation for the future. In this way they take hold of what life really is.

1 Timothy 6:18–19

We understand what love is when we realize that Christ gave his life for us. That means we must give our lives for other believers. Now, suppose a person has enough to live on and notices another believer in need. How can God's love be in that person if he doesn't bother to help the other believer?

1 John 3:16–17

Goodness

Trust the Lord, and do good things.
Live in the land, and practice being faithful.

Psalm 37:3

In the same way let your light shine in front of people. Then they will see the good that you do and praise your Father in heaven.

Matthew 5:16

Besides, God will give you his constantly overflowing kindness. Then, when you always have everything you need, you can do more and more good things.

2 Corinthians 9:8

God has made us what we are. He has created us in Christ Jesus to live lives filled with good works that he has prepared for us to do.

Ephesians 2:10

Don't forget to do good things for others and to share what you have with them. These are the kinds of sacrifices that please God.

Hebrews 13:16

Not everything that the world offers—physical gratification, greed, and extravagant lifestyles—comes from the Father. It comes from the world, and the world and its evil desires are passing away. But the person who does what God wants lives forever.

1 John 2:16–17

Good Stewardship

The Lord asked, "Who, then, is the faithful, skilled manager that the master will put in charge of giving the other servants their share of food at the right time? That servant will be blessed if his master finds him doing this job when he comes."

Luke 12:42–43

Whoever can be trusted with very little can also be trusted with a lot. Whoever is dishonest with very little is dishonest with a lot. Therefore, if you can't be trusted with wealth that is often used dishonestly, who will trust you with wealth that is real? If you can't be trusted with someone else's wealth, who will give you your own?

A servant cannot serve two masters. He will hate the first master and love the second, or he will be devoted to the first and despise the second. You cannot serve God and wealth.

Luke 16:10–13

People should think of us as servants of Christ and managers who are entrusted with God's mysteries. Managers are required to be trustworthy.

1 Corinthians 4:1–2

Each of you as a good manager must use the gift that God has given you to serve others. Whoever speaks must speak God's words. Whoever serves must serve with the strength God supplies so that in every way God receives glory through Jesus Christ. Glory and power belong to Jesus Christ forever and ever! Amen.

1 Peter 4:10–11

Gracious Speech

O LORD, set a guard at my mouth.
  Keep watch over the door of my lips.

Psalm 141:3

The words of wicked people are a deadly ambush,
  but the words of decent people rescue.

Proverbs 12:6

Pleasant words are like honey from a honeycomb—
  sweet to the spirit and healthy for the body.

Proverbs 16:24

Whoever loves a pure heart and whoever speaks
    graciously
  has a king as his friend.

Proverbs 22:11

Good people do the good that is in them. But evil people do the evil that is in them. The things people say come from inside them.

Luke 6:45

Don't say anything that would hurt another person. Instead, speak only what is good so that you can give help wherever it is needed. That way, what you say will help those who hear you.

Ephesians 4:29

Everything you say should be kind and well thought out so that you know how to answer everyone.

Colossians 4:6

Honesty

Who may go up the LORD's mountain?
Who may stand in his holy place?
  The one who has clean hands and a pure heart
    and does not long for what is false
      or lie when he is under oath.
  This person will receive a blessing from the LORD
    and righteousness from God, his savior.

Psalm 24:3–5

Which of you wants a full life?
Who would like to live long enough to enjoy good
    things?
  Keep your tongue from saying evil things
    and your lips from speaking deceitful things.

Psalm 34:12–13

Whoever lives honestly will live securely,
  but whoever lives dishonestly will be found out.

Proverbs 10:9

The word of truth lasts forever,
  but lies last only a moment.

Proverbs 12:19

Lips that lie are disgusting to the LORD,
   but honest people are his delight.

Proverbs 12:22

Better a few possessions gained honestly
   than many gained through injustice.

Proverbs 16:8

Better to be a poor person who lives innocently
   than to be one who talks dishonestly and is a fool.

Proverbs 19:1

Giving a straight answer is like a kiss on the lips.

Proverbs 24:26

The person who does what is right and speaks the
      truth will live.
   He rejects getting rich by extortion and refuses to
      take bribes.
   He refuses to listen to those who are plotting
      murders.
   He doesn't look for evil things to do.
This person will live on high.
   His stronghold will be a fortress made of rock.
      He will have plenty of food
         and a dependable supply of water.

Isaiah 33:15–16

Finally, brothers and sisters, keep your thoughts on whatever is right or deserves praise: things that are true, honorable, fair, pure, acceptable, or commendable. Practice what you've learned and received from me, what you heard and saw me do. Then the God who gives this peace will be with you.

Philippians 4:8–9

Don't lie to each other. You've gotten rid of the person you used to be and the life you used to live, and you've become a new person. This new person is continually renewed in knowledge to be like its Creator.

Colossians 3:9–10

Integrity

I know, my God, that you examine hearts and delight in honesty. With an honest heart I have willingly offered all these things. I've been overjoyed to see your people here offering so willingly to you.

1 Chronicles 29:17

O Lord, who may stay in your tent?
Who may live on your holy mountain?
　　The one who walks with integrity,
　　　　does what is righteous,
　　　　and speaks the truth within his heart.

Psalm 15:1–2

You defend my integrity,
　　and you set me in your presence forever.

Psalm 41:12

The Lord God is a sun and shield.
The Lord grants favor and honor.
He does not hold back any blessing
　　from those who live innocently.

Psalm 84:11

Blessed are those whose lives have integrity,
  those who follow the teachings of the Lord.

Psalm 119:1

He has reserved priceless wisdom for decent
    people.
He is a shield for those who walk in integrity
  in order to guard those on paths of justice
    and to watch over the way of his godly ones.

Proverbs 2:7–8

Integrity guides decent people,
  but hypocrisy leads treacherous people to ruin.

Proverbs 11:3

A righteous person lives on the basis of his integrity.
  Blessed are his children after he is gone.

Proverbs 20:7

Because of this, make every effort to add integrity to your faith; and to integrity add knowledge; to knowledge add self-control; to self-control add endurance; to endurance add godliness; to godliness add Christian affection; and to Christian affection add love. If you have these qualities and they are increasing, it demonstrates that your knowledge about our Lord Jesus Christ is living and productive. If these qualities aren't present in your life, you're shortsighted and have forgotten that you were cleansed from your past sins.

2 Peter 1:5–9

Kindness

A merciful person helps himself,
    but a cruel person hurts himself.

Proverbs 11:17

Whoever oppresses the poor insults his maker,
    but whoever is kind to the needy honors him.

Proverbs 14:31

Whoever has pity on the poor lends to the LORD,
    and he will repay him for his good deed.

Proverbs 19:17

Always do for other people everything you want them to do for you. That is the meaning of Moses' Teachings and the Prophets.

Matthew 7:12

I can guarantee this truth: Whoever gives any of my humble followers a cup of cold water because that person is my disciple will certainly never lose his reward.

Matthew 10:42

Be kind to each other, sympathetic, forgiving each other as God has forgiven you through Christ.

Imitate God, since you are the children he loves. Live in love as Christ also loved us. He gave his life for us as an offering and sacrifice, a soothing aroma to God.

Ephesians 4:32–5:2

As holy people whom God has chosen and loved, be sympathetic, kind, humble, gentle, and patient.

Colossians 3:12

Love

Love the LORD your God with all your heart, with all your soul, and with all your strength.

Deuteronomy 6:5

Rather, love your enemies, help them, and lend to them without expecting to get anything back. Then you will have a great reward. You will be the children of the Most High God. After all, he is kind to unthankful and evil people.

Luke 6:35

God didn't give us a cowardly spirit but a spirit of power, love, and good judgment.

2 Timothy 1:7

You are doing right if you obey this law from the highest authority: "Love your neighbor as you love yourself."

James 2:8

Above all, love each other warmly, because love covers many sins.

1 Peter 4:8

Dear friends, we must love each other because love comes from God. Everyone who loves has been born from God and knows God.

1 John 4:7

No one has ever seen God. If we love each other, God lives in us, and his love is perfected in us.

1 John 4:12

We love because God loved us first.

1 John 4:19

Peace

Hate starts quarrels,
    but love covers every wrong.

Proverbs 10:12

When a person's ways are pleasing to the LORD,
    he makes even his enemies to be at peace with
        him.

Proverbs 16:7

Avoiding a quarrel is honorable.
    After all, any stubborn fool can start a fight.

Proverbs 20:3

Blessed are those who make peace.
    They will be called God's children.

Matthew 5:9

Now that we have God's approval by faith, we have
peace with God because of what our Lord Jesus Christ has
done. Through Christ we can approach God and stand in
his favor. So we brag because of our confidence that we
will receive glory from God.

Romans 5:1–2

Brothers and sisters, I encourage all of you in the name of our Lord Jesus Christ to agree with each other and not to split into opposing groups. I want you to be united in your understanding and opinions.

1 Corinthians 1:10

God's purpose was that the body should not be divided but rather that all of its parts should feel the same concern for each other. If one part of the body suffers, all the other parts share its suffering. If one part is praised, all the others share in its happiness.

1 Corinthians 12:25–26

I, a prisoner in the Lord, encourage you to live the kind of life which proves that God has called you. Be humble and gentle in every way. Be patient with each other and lovingly accept each other. Through the peace that ties you together, do your best to maintain the unity that the Spirit gives.

Ephesians 4:1–3

As holy people whom God has chosen and loved, be sympathetic, kind, humble, gentle, and patient. Put up with each other, and forgive each other if anyone has a complaint. Forgive as the Lord forgave you. Above all, be loving. This ties everything together perfectly. Also, let Christ's peace control you. God has called you into this peace by bringing you into one body. Be thankful.

Colossians 3:12–15

However, the wisdom that comes from above is first of all pure. Then it is peaceful, gentle, obedient, filled with mercy and good deeds, impartial, and sincere.

James 3:17

Praise and Worship

I waited patiently for the LORD.
 He turned to me and heard my cry for help.
 He pulled me out of a horrible pit,
  out of the mud and clay.
 He set my feet on a rock
  and made my steps secure.
 He placed a new song in my mouth,
  a song of praise to our God.
   Many will see this and worship.
   They will trust the LORD.

Psalm 40:1–3

Whoever offers thanks as a sacrifice honors me.
I will let everyone who continues in my way
 see the salvation that comes from God.

Psalm 50:23

So I will thank you as long as I live.
 I will lift up my hands to pray in your name.
You satisfy my soul with the richest foods.
 My mouth will sing your praise with joyful lips.

Psalm 63:4–5

Come, let's worship and bow down.
Let's kneel in front of the LORD, our maker,
because he is our God
and we are the people in his care,
the flock that he leads.

Psalm 95:6–7

With my mouth I will give many thanks to the
LORD.
I will praise him among many people,
because he stands beside needy people
to save them from those who would condemn
them to death.

Psalm 109:30–31

Let them praise his name with dancing.
Let them make music to him with tambourines and
lyres,
because the LORD takes pleasure in his people.
He crowns those who are oppressed with
victory.
Let godly people triumph in glory.
Let them sing for joy on their beds.

Psalm 149:3–5

Then young women will rejoice and dance
along with young men and old men.
I will turn their mourning into joy.
I will comfort them.
I will give them joy in place of their sorrow.

Jeremiah 31:13

Then I will give all people pure lips
   to worship the Lord
      and to serve him with one purpose.

Zephaniah 3:9

Indeed, the time is coming, and it is now here, when the true worshipers will worship the Father in spirit and truth. The Father is looking for people like that to worship him. God is a spirit. Those who worship him must worship in spirit and truth.

John 4:23–24

Brothers and sisters, in view of all we have just shared about God's compassion, I encourage you to offer your bodies as living sacrifices, dedicated to God and pleasing to him. This kind of worship is appropriate for you.

Romans 12:1

Purity

How can a young person keep his life pure?
He can do it by holding on to your word.

Psalm 119:9

Blessed are those whose thoughts are pure.
They will see God.

Matthew 5:8

You were taught to change the way you were living.
The person you used to be will ruin you through desires
that deceive you. However, you were taught to have a new
attitude. You were also taught to become a new person
created to be like God, truly righteous and holy.

Ephesians 4:22–24

It trains us to avoid ungodly lives filled with worldly
desires so that we can live self-controlled, moral, and godly
lives in this present world. At the same time we can expect
what we hope for—the appearance of the glory of our great
God and Savior, Jesus Christ.

Titus 2:12–13

However, the wisdom that comes from above is first of all pure. Then it is peaceful, gentle, obedient, filled with mercy and good deeds, impartial, and sincere.

James 3:17

But if we live in the light in the same way that God is in the light, we have a relationship with each other. And the blood of his Son Jesus cleanses us from every sin.

1 John 1:7

Don't love the world and what it offers. Those who love the world don't have the Father's love in them. Not everything that the world offers—physical gratification, greed, and extravagant lifestyles—comes from the Father. It comes from the world, and the world and its evil desires are passing away. But the person who does what God wants lives forever.

1 John 2:15–17

Righteousness

He doesn't take his eyes off righteous people.
He seats them on thrones with kings to honor them
    forever.

Job 36:7

He renews my soul.
He guides me along the paths of righteousness
    for the sake of his name.

Psalm 23:3

He will make your righteousness shine like a light,
    your just cause like the noonday sun.

Psalm 37:6

The mouth of the righteous person reflects on
    wisdom.
    His tongue speaks what is fair.
The teachings of his God are in his heart.
    His feet do not slip.

Psalm 37:30–31

The righteousness of innocent people makes their
    road smooth,
    but wicked people fall by their own wickedness.

Proverbs 11:5

The fruit of a righteous person is a tree of life,
    and a winner of souls is wise.

Proverbs 11:30

Blessed are those who hunger and thirst for God's
    approval.
    They will be satisfied.

Matthew 5:6

The Lord's eyes are on those who do what he
    approves.
    His ears hear their prayer.
    The Lord confronts those who do evil.

1 Peter 3:12

Self-Control

Whoever controls his mouth protects his own life.
Whoever has a big mouth comes to ruin.

Proverbs 13:3

A wise person's heart controls his speech,
and what he says helps others learn.
Pleasant words are like honey from a honeycomb—
sweet to the spirit and healthy for the body.

Proverbs 16:23–24

Whoever guards his mouth and his tongue keeps himself
out of trouble.

Proverbs 21:23

If you live by your corrupt nature, you are going to die.
But if you use your spiritual nature to put to death the evil
activities of the body, you will live. Certainly, all who are
guided by God's Spirit are God's children.

Romans 8:13–14

There isn't any temptation that you have experienced which is unusual for humans. God, who faithfully keeps his promises, will not allow you to be tempted beyond your power to resist. But when you are tempted, he will also give you the ability to endure the temptation as your way of escape.

1 Corinthians 10:13

It trains us to avoid ungodly lives filled with worldly desires so that we can live self-controlled, moral, and godly lives in this present world. At the same time we can expect what we hope for—the appearance of the glory of our great God and Savior, Jesus Christ.

Titus 2:12–13

Therefore, your minds must be clear and ready for action. Place your confidence completely in what God's kindness will bring you when Jesus Christ appears again.

1 Peter 1:13

The end of everything is near. Therefore, practice self-control, and keep your minds clear so that you can pray.

1 Peter 4:7

Because of this, make every effort to add integrity to your faith; and to integrity add knowledge; to knowledge add self-control; to self-control add endurance; to endurance add godliness; to godliness add Christian affection; and to Christian affection add love.

2 Peter 1:5–7

Service

Those who serve me must follow me. My servants will be with me wherever I will be. If people serve me, the Father will honor them.

John 12:26

You didn't choose me, but I chose you. I have appointed you to go, to produce fruit that will last, and to ask the Father in my name to give you whatever you ask for.

John 15:16

He also gave apostles, prophets, missionaries, as well as pastors and teachers as gifts to his church. Their purpose is to prepare God's people to serve and to build up the body of Christ.

Ephesians 4:11–12

Serve eagerly as if you were serving your heavenly master and not merely serving human masters. You know that your heavenly master will reward all of us for whatever good we do, whether we're slaves or free people.

Ephesians 6:7–8

Whatever you do, do it wholeheartedly as though you were working for your real master and not merely for humans. You know that your real master will give you an inheritance as your reward. It is Christ, your real master, whom you are serving.

Colossians 3:23–24

Each of you as a good manager must use the gift that God has given you to serve others. Whoever speaks must speak God's words. Whoever serves must serve with the strength God supplies so that in every way God receives glory through Jesus Christ. Glory and power belong to Jesus Christ forever and ever! Amen.

1 Peter 4:10–11

Sincerity

We are proud that our conscience is clear. We are proud of the way that we have lived in this world. We have lived with a God-given holiness and sincerity, especially toward you. It was not by human wisdom that we have lived but by God's kindness.

2 Corinthians 1:12

At least we don't go around selling an impure word of God like many others. The opposite is true. As Christ's spokesmen and in God's presence, we speak the pure message that comes from God.

2 Corinthians 2:17

Slaves, obey your earthly masters with proper respect. Be as sincere as you are when you obey Christ.

Ephesians 6:5

My goal in giving you this order is for love to flow from a pure heart, from a clear conscience, and from a sincere faith.

1 Timothy 1:5

We have a superior priest in charge of God's house. We have been sprinkled with his blood to free us from a guilty conscience, and our bodies have been washed with clean water. So we must continue to come to him with a sincere heart and strong faith. We must continue to hold firmly to our declaration of faith. The one who made the promise is faithful.

Hebrews 10:21–23

However, the wisdom that comes from above is first of all pure. Then it is peaceful, gentle, obedient, filled with mercy and good deeds, impartial, and sincere.

James 3:17

Love each other with a warm love that comes from the heart. After all, you have purified yourselves by obeying the truth. As a result you have a sincere love for each other.

1 Peter 1:22

Strong Values

However, be careful, and watch yourselves closely so that you don't forget the things which you have seen with your own eyes. Don't let them fade from your memory as long as you live. Teach them to your children and grandchildren.

Deuteronomy 4:9

Who may go up the LORD's mountain?
Who may stand in his holy place?
　　The one who has clean hands and a pure heart
　　　　and does not long for what is false
　　　　or lie when he is under oath.
　　This person will receive a blessing from the LORD
　　　　and righteousness from God, his savior.

Psalm 24:3–5

He said to all of them, "Those who want to come with me must say no to the things they want, pick up their crosses every day, and follow me. Those who want to save their lives will lose them. But those who lose their lives for me will save them. What good does it do for people to win the whole world but lose their lives by destroying them?"

Luke 9:23–25

He told the people, "Be careful to guard yourselves from every kind of greed. Life is not about having a lot of material possessions."

Luke 12:15

Finally, brothers and sisters, keep your thoughts on whatever is right or deserves praise: things that are true, honorable, fair, pure, acceptable, or commendable.

Philippians 4:8

Keep your mind on things above, not on worldly things.

Colossians 3:2

Don't lie to each other. You've gotten rid of the person you used to be and the life you used to live, and you've become a new person. This new person is continually renewed in knowledge to be like its Creator.

Colossians 3:9–10

It trains us to avoid ungodly lives filled with worldly desires so that we can live self-controlled, moral, and godly lives in this present world. At the same time we can expect what we hope for—the appearance of the glory of our great God and Savior, Jesus Christ.

Titus 2:12–13

Don't love the world and what it offers. Those who love the world don't have the Father's love in them. Not everything that the world offers—physical gratification, greed, and extravagant lifestyles—comes from the Father. It comes from the world, and the world and its evil desires are passing away. But the person who does what God wants lives forever.

1 John 2:15–17

True Beauty

But the LORD told Samuel, "Don't look at his appearance or how tall he is, because I have rejected him. God does not see as humans see. Humans look at outward appearances, but the LORD looks into the heart."

1 Samuel 16:7

Charm is deceptive, and beauty evaporates,
　　but a woman who has the fear of the LORD should
　　be praised.
Reward her for what she has done,
　　and let her achievements praise her at the city
　　gates.

Proverbs 31:30–31

I want women to show their beauty by dressing in appropriate clothes that are modest and respectable. Their beauty will be shown by what they do, not by their hairstyles or the gold jewelry, pearls, or expensive clothes they wear. This is what is proper for women who claim to have reverence for God.

1 Timothy 2:9–10

Wives must not let their beauty be something external. Beauty doesn't come from hairstyles, gold jewelry, or clothes. Rather, beauty is something internal that can't be destroyed. Beauty expresses itself in a gentle and quiet attitude which God considers precious.

1 Peter 3:3–4

God Promises That He
Will Be Faithful to . . .

Answer Prayer

However, if my people, who are called by my name,
   will humble themselves,
      pray, search for me, and turn from their evil ways,
then I will hear their prayer from heaven, forgive
      their sins,
   and heal their country.

                                          2 Chronicles 7:14

But I call on God,
   and the LORD saves me.
Morning, noon, and night I complain and groan,
   and he listens to my voice.

                                          Psalm 55:16–17

When I am in trouble, I call out to you
   because you answer me.

                                          Psalm 86:7

When you call to me, I will answer you.
  I will be with you when you are in trouble.
  I will save you and honor you.
  I will satisfy you with a long life.
  I will show you how I will save you.

Psalm 91:15–16

Call to me, and I will answer you. I will tell you great and mysterious things that you do not know.

Jeremiah 33:3

When you pray, go to your room and close the door. Pray privately to your Father who is with you. Your Father sees what you do in private. He will reward you.

Matthew 6:6

Ask, and you will receive. Search, and you will find. Knock, and the door will be opened for you. Everyone who asks will receive. The one who searches will find, and for the one who knocks, the door will be opened.

Matthew 7:7–8

Have faith that you will receive whatever you ask for in prayer.

Matthew 21:22

Jesus said to them, "Have faith in God! I can guarantee this truth: This is what will be done for someone who doesn't doubt but believes what he says will happen: He can say to this mountain, 'Be uprooted and thrown into the sea,' and it will be done for him. That's why I tell you to have faith that you have already received whatever you pray for, and it will be yours."

Mark 11:22–24

When that day comes, you won't ask me any more questions. I can guarantee this truth: If you ask the Father for anything in my name, he will give it to you. So far you haven't asked for anything in my name. Ask and you will receive so that you can be completely happy.

John 16:23–24

Always be joyful in the Lord! I'll say it again: Be joyful! Let everyone know how considerate you are. The Lord is near. Never worry about anything. But in every situation let God know what you need in prayers and requests while giving thanks. Then God's peace, which goes beyond anything we can imagine, will guard your thoughts and emotions through Christ Jesus.

Philippians 4:4–7

If any of you are having trouble, pray. If you are happy, sing psalms. If you are sick, call for the church leaders. Have them pray for you and anoint you with olive oil in the name of the Lord. (Prayers offered in faith will save those who are sick, and the Lord will cure them.) If you have sinned, you will be forgiven. So admit your sins to each other, and pray for each other so that you will be healed.

James 5:13–16

We are confident that God listens to us if we ask for anything that has his approval. We know that he listens to our requests. So we know that we already have what we ask him for.

1 John 5:14–15

Disciple Us

Therefore, everyone who hears what I say and obeys it will be like a wise person who built a house on rock. Rain poured, and floods came. Winds blew and beat against that house. But it did not collapse, because its foundation was on rock.

Everyone who hears what I say but doesn't obey it will be like a foolish person who built a house on sand. Rain poured, and floods came. Winds blew and struck that house. It collapsed, and the result was a total disaster.

Matthew 7:24–27

Jesus spoke to the Pharisees again. He said, "I am the light of the world. Whoever follows me will have a life filled with light and will never live in the dark."

John 8:12

So Jesus said to those Jews who believed in him, "If you live by what I say, you are truly my disciples. You will know the truth, and the truth will set you free."

John 8:31–32

My sheep respond to my voice, and I know who they are. They follow me, and I give them eternal life. They will never be lost, and no one will tear them away from me.

John 10:27–28

Those who serve me must follow me. My servants will be with me wherever I will be. If people serve me, the Father will honor them.

John 12:26

However, the helper, the Holy Spirit, whom the Father will send in my name, will teach you everything. He will remind you of everything that I have ever told you.

John 14:26

You give glory to my Father when you produce a lot of fruit and therefore show that you are my disciples.

John 15:8

On earth we have fathers who disciplined us, and we respect them. Shouldn't we place ourselves under the authority of God, the father of spirits, so that we will live? For a short time our fathers disciplined us as they thought best. Yet, God disciplines us for our own good so that we can become holy like him.

Hebrews 12:9–10

Give Eternal Life

But I know that my defender lives,
and afterwards, he will rise on the earth.
Even after my skin has been stripped off my body,
I will see God in my own flesh.

Job 19:25–26

Certainly, goodness and mercy will stay close to me
all the days of my life,
and I will remain in the Lord's house for days
without end.

Psalm 23:6

God loved the world this way: He gave his only Son
so that everyone who believes in him will not die but will
have eternal life.

John 3:16

I can guarantee this truth: Those who listen to what I
say and believe in the one who sent me will have eternal
life. They won't be judged because they have already passed
from death to life.

John 5:24

Jesus told them, "I can guarantee this truth: If you don't eat the flesh of the Son of Man and drink his blood, you don't have the source of life in you. Those who eat my flesh and drink my blood have eternal life, and I will bring them back to life on the last day."

John 6:53–54

My sheep respond to my voice, and I know who they are. They follow me, and I give them eternal life. They will never be lost, and no one will tear them away from me.

John 10:27–28

Jesus said to her, "I am the one who brings people back to life, and I am life itself. Those who believe in me will live even if they die. Everyone who lives and believes in me will never die. Do you believe that?"

John 11:25–26

Don't be troubled. Believe in God, and believe in me. My Father's house has many rooms. If that were not true, would I have told you that I'm going to prepare a place for you? If I go to prepare a place for you, I will come again. Then I will bring you into my presence so that you will be where I am.

John 14:1–3

This is eternal life: to know you, the only true God, and Jesus Christ, whom you sent.

John 17:3

Now you have been freed from sin and have become God's slaves. This results in a holy life and, finally, in everlasting life. The payment for sin is death, but the gift that God freely gives is everlasting life found in Christ Jesus our Lord.

Romans 6:22–23

It's clear that we don't live to honor ourselves, and we don't die to honor ourselves. If we live, we honor the Lord, and if we die, we honor the Lord. So whether we live or die, we belong to the Lord.

Romans 14:7–8

As a result, God in his kindness has given us his approval and we have become heirs who have the confidence that we have everlasting life.

Titus 3:7

This is the testimony: God has given us eternal life, and this life is found in his Son. The person who has the Son has this life. The person who doesn't have the Son of God doesn't have this life.

1 John 5:11–12

Give Us Joy

You make the path of life known to me.
  Complete joy is in your presence.
    Pleasures are by your side forever.

Psalm 16:11

You have changed my sobbing into dancing.
You have removed my sackcloth and clothed me with
    joy
  so that my soul may praise you with music and
    not be silent.
O LORD my God, I will give thanks to you forever.

Psalm 30:11–12

You made me find joy in what you have done,
    O LORD.
I will sing joyfully about the works of your hands.

Psalm 92:4

Those who cry while they plant
  will joyfully sing while they harvest.

Psalm 126:5

The people ransomed by the LORD will return.
They will come to Zion singing with joy.
Everlasting happiness will be on their heads as
a crown.
They will be glad and joyful.
They will have no sorrow or grief.

Isaiah 35:10

Sing with joy, you heavens!
Rejoice, you earth!
Break into shouts of joy, you mountains!
The LORD has comforted his people
and will have compassion on his humble
people.

Isaiah 49:13

You will go out with joy and be led out in peace.
The mountains and the hills
will break into songs of joy in your presence,
and all the trees will clap their hands.

Isaiah 55:12

I will find joy in the LORD.
I will delight in my God.
He has dressed me in the clothes of salvation.
He has wrapped me in the robe of righteousness
like a bridegroom with a priest's turban,
like a bride with her jewels.

Isaiah 61:10

Always be joyful in the Lord! I'll say it again: Be joyful! Let everyone know how considerate you are. The Lord is near. Never worry about anything. But in every situation let God know what you need in prayers and requests while giving thanks. Then God's peace, which goes beyond anything we can imagine, will guard your thoughts and emotions through Christ Jesus.

Philippians 4:4–7

Give Us Victory

The LORD is my strength and my shield.
My heart trusted him, so I received help.
My heart is triumphant; I give thanks to him with
    my song.
The LORD is the strength of his people
  and a fortress for the victory of his Messiah.

Psalm 28:7–8

Horses are not a guarantee for victory.
  Their great strength cannot help someone escape.
The LORD's eyes are on those who fear him,
  on those who wait with hope for his mercy
    to rescue their souls from death
      and keep them alive during a famine.

Psalm 33:17–19

The victory for righteous people comes from the
LORD.
He is their fortress in times of trouble.
The LORD helps them and rescues them.
He rescues them from wicked people.
He saves them because they have taken refuge in
him.

Psalm 37:39–40

No wisdom, no understanding, and no advice
can stand up against the LORD.
The horse is made ready for the day of battle,
but the victory belongs to the LORD.

Proverbs 21:30–31

I have sinned against the LORD.
So I will endure his fury
until he takes up my cause and wins my case.
He will bring me into the light,
and I will see his victory.

Micah 7:9

I've told you this so that my peace will be with you. In
the world you'll have trouble. But cheer up! I have overcome
the world.

John 16:33

What will separate us from the love Christ has for us?
Can trouble, distress, persecution, hunger, nakedness, dan-
ger, or violent death separate us from his love? . . . The
one who loves us gives us an overwhelming victory in all
these difficulties.

Romans 8:35, 37

Thank God that he gives us the victory through our Lord Jesus Christ.

1 Corinthians 15:57

But I thank God, who always leads us in victory because of Christ. Wherever we go, God uses us to make clear what it means to know Christ. It's like a fragrance that fills the air.

2 Corinthians 2:14

Who wins the victory over the world? Isn't it the person who believes that Jesus is the Son of God?

1 John 5:5

I will allow everyone who wins the victory to sit with me on my throne, as I have won the victory and have sat down with my Father on his throne.

Revelation 3:21

Guide Us

He renews my soul.
He guides me along the paths of righteousness
for the sake of his name.

Psalm 23:3

The LORD is good and decent.
That is why he teaches sinners the way they
should live.
He leads humble people to do what is right,
and he teaches them his way.

Psalm 25:8–9

The LORD says,
"I will instruct you.
I will teach you the way that you should go.
I will advise you as my eyes watch over you."

Psalm 32:8

If I climb upward on the rays of the morning sun
or land on the most distant shore of the sea where
the sun sets,
even there your hand would guide me
and your right hand would hold on to me.

Psalm 139:9–10

Trust the LORD with all your heart,
  and do not rely on your own understanding.
In all your ways acknowledge him,
  and he will make your paths smooth.

Proverbs 3:5–6

You will hear a voice behind you saying, "This is the way. Follow it, whether it turns to the right or to the left."

Isaiah 30:21

The LORD will continually guide you
  and satisfy you even in sun-baked places.
He will strengthen your bones.
  You will become like a watered garden
    and like a spring whose water does not stop
      flowing.

Isaiah 58:11

When the Spirit of Truth comes, he will guide you into the full truth. He won't speak on his own. He will speak what he hears and will tell you about things to come.

John 16:13

If any of you needs wisdom to know what you should do, you should ask God, and he will give it to you. God is generous to everyone and doesn't find fault with them.

James 1:5

Help Us

You have seen it; yes, you have taken note of trouble
and grief
and placed them under your control.
The victim entrusts himself to you.
You alone have been the helper of orphans.

Psalm 10:14

The LORD is my strength and my shield.
My heart trusted him, so I received help.
My heart is triumphant; I give thanks to him with
my song.

Psalm 28:7

We wait for the LORD.
He is our help and our shield.

Psalm 33:20

God is our refuge and strength,
an ever-present help in times of trouble.

Psalm 46:1

God is my helper!
The Lord is the provider for my life.

Psalm 54:4

But I am oppressed and needy.
O God, come to me quickly.
You are my help and my savior.
O Lord, do not delay!

Psalm 70:5

The Lord is on my side as my helper.
I will see the defeat of those who hate me.

Psalm 118:7

Blessed are those who receive help from the God of
Jacob.
Their hope rests on the Lord their God.

Psalm 146:5

At the same time the Spirit also helps us in our weakness, because we don't know how to pray for what we need. But the Spirit intercedes along with our groans that cannot be expressed in words.

Romans 8:26

Because Jesus experienced temptation when he suffered, he is able to help others when they are tempted.

Hebrews 2:18

So we can confidently say,
"The Lord is my helper.
I will not be afraid.
What can mortals do to me?"

Hebrews 13:6

God Promises
to Strengthen Women
in Their . . .

Daily Walk with Him

O Lord, who may stay in your tent?
Who may live on your holy mountain?
   The one who walks with integrity,
     does what is righteous,
     and speaks the truth within his heart.

                    Psalm 15:1–2

You make a wide path for me to walk on
   so that my feet do not slip.

                    Psalm 18:36

You have rescued me from death.
You have kept my feet from stumbling
   so that I could walk in your presence, in the light
     of life.

                    Psalm 56:13

Blessed are the people who know how to praise you.
   They walk in the light of your presence, O Lord.
   They find joy in your name all day long.
   They are joyful in your righteousness
     because you are the glory of their strength.

                    Psalm 89:15–17

You saved me from death.
You saved my eyes from tears and my feet from
    stumbling.
I will walk in the LORD's presence in this world of
    the living.

Psalm 116:8–9

Those who love their lives will destroy them, and those who hate their lives in this world will guard them for everlasting life. Those who serve me must follow me. My servants will be with me wherever I will be. If people serve me, the Father will honor them.

John 12:25–26

Don't become like the people of this world. Instead, change the way you think. Then you will always be able to determine what God really wants—what is good, pleasing, and perfect.

Romans 12:2

Those who belong to Christ Jesus have crucified their corrupt nature along with its passions and desires. If we live by our spiritual nature, then our lives need to conform to our spiritual nature.

Galatians 5:24–25

We ask this so that you will live the kind of lives that prove you belong to the Lord. Then you will want to please him in every way as you grow in producing every kind of good work by this knowledge about God.

Colossians 1:10

You received Christ Jesus the Lord, so continue to live as Christ's people. Sink your roots in him and build on him. Be strengthened by the faith that you were taught, and overflow with thanksgiving.

Colossians 2:6–7

Decision Making

Blessed is the person who does not
   follow the advice of wicked people,
      take the path of sinners,
         or join the company of mockers.
Rather, he delights in the teachings of the LORD
   and reflects on his teachings day and night.

Psalm 1:1–2

I will praise the LORD, who advises me.
   My conscience warns me at night.

Psalm 16:7

The LORD says,
   "I will instruct you.
   I will teach you the way that you should go.
   I will advise you as my eyes watch over you."

Psalm 32:8

Yet, I am always with you.
   You hold on to my right hand.
      With your advice you guide me,
         and in the end you will take me to glory.

Psalm 73:23–24

This is what the LORD says:
Stand at the crossroads and look.
Ask which paths are the old, reliable paths.
Ask which way leads to blessings.
Live that way, and find a resting place for
yourselves.
But you said that you wouldn't live that way.

Jeremiah 6:16

However, the helper, the Holy Spirit, whom the Father will send in my name, will teach you everything. He will remind you of everything that I have ever told you.

John 14:26

"Who has known the mind of the Lord
so that he can teach him?"
However, we have the mind of Christ.

1 Corinthians 2:16

I pray that the glorious Father, the God of our Lord Jesus Christ, would give you a spirit of wisdom and revelation as you come to know Christ better. Then you will have deeper insight. You will know the confidence that he calls you to have and the glorious wealth that God's people will inherit. You will also know the unlimited greatness of his power as it works with might and strength for us, the believers.

Ephesians 1:17–19

If any of you needs wisdom to know what you should do, you should ask God, and he will give it to you. God is generous to everyone and doesn't find fault with them. When you ask for something, don't have any doubts. A person who has doubts is like a wave that is blown by the wind and tossed by the sea.

James 1:5–6

However, the wisdom that comes from above is first of all pure. Then it is peaceful, gentle, obedient, filled with mercy and good deeds, impartial, and sincere.

James 3:17

We know that the Son of God has come and has given us understanding so that we know the real God. We are in the one who is real, his Son Jesus Christ. This Jesus Christ is the real God and eternal life.

1 John 5:20

Priorities

Be happy with the LORD,
    and he will give you the desires of your heart.

Psalm 37:4

Whoever pursues righteousness and mercy
    will find life, righteousness, and honor.

Proverbs 21:21

Stop storing up treasures for yourselves on earth, where moths and rust destroy and thieves break in and steal. Instead, store up treasures for yourselves in heaven, where moths and rust don't destroy and thieves don't break in and steal. Your heart will be where your treasure is.

Matthew 6:19–21

But first, be concerned about his kingdom and what has his approval. Then all these things will be provided for you.

Matthew 6:33

Then Jesus said to his disciples, "Those who want to come with me must say no to the things they want, pick up their crosses, and follow me. Those who want to save their lives will lose them. But those who lose their lives for me will find them."

Matthew 16:24–25

We don't look for things that can be seen but for things that can't be seen. Things that can be seen are only temporary. But things that can't be seen last forever.

2 Corinthians 4:18

You suffered with prisoners. You were cheerful even though your possessions were stolen, since you know that you have a better and more permanent possession.

Hebrews 10:34

We must focus on Jesus, the source and goal of our faith. He saw the joy ahead of him, so he endured death on the cross and ignored the disgrace it brought him. Then he received the highest position in heaven, the one next to the throne of God.

Hebrews 12:2

Spiritual Growth

Never stop reciting these teachings. You must think about them night and day so that you will faithfully do everything written in them. Only then will you prosper and succeed.

Joshua 1:8

The LORD says,
"I will instruct you.
I will teach you the way that you should go.
I will advise you as my eyes watch over you."

Psalm 32:8

O God, you are my God.
At dawn I search for you.
My soul thirsts for you.
My body longs for you
in a dry, parched land where there is no
water.
So I look for you in the holy place
to see your power and your glory.

Psalm 63:1–2

I am the vine. You are the branches. Those who live in me while I live in them will produce a lot of fruit. But you can't produce anything without me.

John 15:5

Then we will no longer be little children, tossed and carried about by all kinds of teachings that change like the wind. We will no longer be influenced by people who use cunning and clever strategies to lead us astray. Instead, as we lovingly speak the truth, we will grow up completely in our relationship to Christ, who is the head.

Ephesians 4:14–15

Desire God's pure word as newborn babies desire milk. Then you will grow in your salvation. Certainly you have tasted that the Lord is good!

1 Peter 2:2–3

Stability and Strength

The LORD is my strength and my song.
>   He is my Savior.
>>   This is my God, and I will praise him,
>>>   my father's God, and I will honor him.

>>>>>   Exodus 15:2

God arms me with strength.
His perfect way sets me free.
>   He makes my feet like those of a deer
>>   and gives me sure footing on high places.

>>>>>   2 Samuel 22:33–34

The LORD is my strength and my shield.
My heart trusted him, so I received help.
My heart is triumphant; I give thanks to him with
>   my song.
The LORD is the strength of his people
>   and a fortress for the victory of his Messiah.

>>>>>   Psalm 28:7–8

God is our refuge and strength,
>   an ever-present help in times of trouble.

>>>>>   Psalm 46:1

My soul waits calmly for God alone.
My salvation comes from him.
He alone is my rock and my savior—my stronghold.
I cannot be severely shaken.

Psalm 62:1–2

Blessed are those who find strength in you.
Their hearts are on the road that leads to you.
As they pass through a valley where balsam
trees grow,
they make it a place of springs.
The early rains cover it with blessings.
Their strength grows as they go along
until each one of them appears
in front of God in Zion.

Psalm 84:5–7

You saved me from death.
You saved my eyes from tears and my feet from
stumbling.
I will walk in the LORD's presence in this world of
the living.

Psalm 116:8–9

Don't be afraid, because I am with you.
Don't be intimidated; I am your God.
I will strengthen you.
I will help you.
I will support you with my victorious right hand.

Isaiah 41:10

Therefore, you don't lack any gift as you wait eagerly for our Lord Jesus Christ to be revealed. He will continue to give you strength until the end so that no one can accuse you of anything on the day of our Lord Jesus Christ.

1 Corinthians 1:7–8

I can do everything through Christ who strengthens me.

Philippians 4:13

Then he will strengthen you to be holy. Then you will be blameless in the presence of our God and Father when our Lord Jesus comes with all God's holy people.

1 Thessalonians 3:13

God, who shows you his kindness and who has called you through Christ Jesus to his eternal glory, will restore you, strengthen you, make you strong, and support you as you suffer for a little while.

1 Peter 5:10

God Keeps His Promises through . . .

Answered Prayer

You will pray to him, and he will listen to you,
   and you will keep your vow to him.

Job 22:27

I call aloud to the LORD,
   and he answers me from his holy mountain.

Psalm 3:4

Get away from me, all you troublemakers,
   because the LORD has heard the sound of my
      crying.
      The LORD has heard my plea for mercy.
      The LORD accepts my prayer.

Psalm 6:8–9

I have called on you because you answer me, O God.
   Turn your ear toward me.
   Hear what I have to say.

Psalm 17:6

Call on me in times of trouble.
 I will rescue you, and you will honor me.

Psalm 50:15

But I call on God,
 and the LORD saves me.
Morning, noon, and night I complain and groan,
 and he listens to my voice.

Psalm 55:16–17

But God has heard me.
 He has paid attention to my prayer.
Thanks be to God,
 who has not rejected my prayer
  or taken away his mercy from me.

Psalm 66:19–20

He will turn his attention to the prayers
 of those who have been abandoned.
He will not despise their prayers.

Psalm 102:17

When I was in trouble, I cried out to the LORD,
 and he answered me.

Psalm 120:1

The LORD is near to everyone who prays to him,
 to every faithful person who prays to him.
He fills the needs of those who fear him.
He hears their cries for help and saves them.

Psalm 145:18–19

The LORD is far from wicked people,
  but he hears the prayers of righteous people.

Proverbs 15:29

Before they call, I will answer.
  While they're still speaking, I will hear.

Isaiah 65:24

I called to the LORD in my distress,
  and he answered me.
From the depths of my watery grave I cried for help,
  and you heard my cry.

Jonah 2:2

When you pray, don't ramble like heathens who think they'll be heard if they talk a lot. Don't be like them. Your Father knows what you need before you ask him.

Matthew 6:7–8

Ask, and you will receive. Search, and you will find. Knock, and the door will be opened for you. Everyone who asks will receive. The one who searches will find, and for the one who knocks, the door will be opened.

Matthew 7:7–8

Have faith that you will receive whatever you ask for in prayer.

Matthew 21:22

That's why I tell you to have faith that you have already received whatever you pray for, and it will be yours.

Mark 11:24

I will do anything you ask the Father in my name so that the Father will be given glory because of the Son. If you ask me to do something, I will do it.

John 14:13–14

So we can go confidently to the throne of God's kindness to receive mercy and find kindness, which will help us at the right time.

Hebrews 4:16

If any of you are having trouble, pray. If you are happy, sing psalms. If you are sick, call for the church leaders. Have them pray for you and anoint you with olive oil in the name of the Lord. (Prayers offered in faith will save those who are sick, and the Lord will cure them.) If you have sinned, you will be forgiven. So admit your sins to each other, and pray for each other so that you will be healed.

Prayers offered by those who have God's approval are effective.

James 5:13–16

The Lord's eyes are on those who do what he
    approves.
  His ears hear their prayer.
  The Lord confronts those who do evil.

1 Peter 3:12

I've written this to those who believe in the Son of God so that they will know that they have eternal life.

We are confident that God listens to us if we ask for anything that has his approval. We know that he listens to our requests. So we know that we already have what we ask him for.

1 John 5:13–15

The Church

Jesus replied, "Simon, son of Jonah, you are blessed! No human revealed this to you, but my Father in heaven revealed it to you. You are Peter, and I can guarantee that on this rock I will build my church. And the gates of hell will not overpower it."

Matthew 16:17–18

Our bodies have many parts, but these parts don't all do the same thing. In the same way, even though we are many individuals, Christ makes us one body and individuals who are connected to each other. God in his kindness gave each of us different gifts. If your gift is speaking what God has revealed, make sure what you say agrees with the Christian faith.

Romans 12:4–6

The body is one unit and yet has many parts. As all the parts form one body, so it is with Christ. By one Spirit we were all baptized into one body. Whether we are Jewish or Greek, slave or free, God gave all of us one Spirit to drink.

1 Corinthians 12:12–13

You are Christ's body and each of you is an individual part of it. In the church God has appointed first apostles, next prophets, third teachers, then those who perform miracles, then those who have the gift of healing, then those who help others, those who are managers, and those who can speak in a number of languages.

1 Corinthians 12:27–28

God has put everything under the control of Christ. He has made Christ the head of everything for the good of the church.

Ephesians 1:22

That is why you are no longer foreigners and outsiders but citizens together with God's people and members of God's family. You are built on the foundation of the apostles and prophets. Christ Jesus himself is the cornerstone. In him all the parts of the building fit together and grow into a holy temple in the Lord. Through him you, also, are being built in the Spirit together with others into a place where God lives.

Ephesians 2:19–22

He also gave apostles, prophets, missionaries, as well as pastors and teachers as gifts to his church. Their purpose is to prepare God's people to serve and to build up the body of Christ. This is to continue until all of us are united in our faith and in our knowledge about God's Son, until we become mature, until we measure up to Christ, who is the standard.

Ephesians 4:11–13

He makes the whole body fit together and unites it through the support of every joint. As each and every part does its job, he makes the body grow so that it builds itself up in love.

Ephesians 4:16

We should not stop gathering together with other believers, as some of you are doing. Instead, we must continue to encourage each other even more as we see the day of the Lord coming.

Hebrews 10:25

However, you are chosen people, a royal priesthood, a holy nation, people who belong to God. You were chosen to tell about the excellent qualities of God, who called you out of darkness into his marvelous light.

1 Peter 2:9

The Family

God places lonely people in families.
He leads prisoners out of prison into productive
lives,
but rebellious people must live in an unproduc-
tive land.

Psalm 68:6

Children are an inheritance from the LORD.
They are a reward from him.
The children born to a man when he is young
are like arrows in the hand of a warrior.
Blessed is the man who has filled his quiver
with them.
He will not be put to shame
when he speaks with his enemies in the
city gate.

Psalm 127:3–5

In the fear of the LORD there is strong confidence,
and his children will have a place of refuge.

Proverbs 14:26

Jesus answered, "Haven't you read that the Creator made them male and female in the beginning and that he said, 'That's why a man will leave his father and mother and will remain united with his wife, and the two will be one'?"

Matthew 19:4–5

Whenever we have the opportunity, we have to do what is good for everyone, especially for the family of believers.

Galatians 6:10

Imitate God, since you are the children he loves. Live in love as Christ also loved us. He gave his life for us as an offering and sacrifice, a soothing aroma to God.

Ephesians 5:1–2

Once you lived in the dark, but now the Lord has filled you with light. Live as children who have light. Light produces everything that is good, that has God's approval, and that is true. Determine which things please the Lord.

Ephesians 5:8–10

Jesus, who makes people holy, and all those who are made holy have the same Father. That is why Jesus isn't ashamed to call them brothers and sisters.

Hebrews 2:11

Consider this: The Father has given us his love. He loves us so much that we are actually called God's dear children. And that's what we are. For this reason the world doesn't recognize us, and it didn't recognize him either.

1 John 3:1

The Holy Spirit

I will give you a new heart and put a new spirit in you. I will remove your stubborn hearts and give you obedient hearts. I will put my Spirit in you. I will enable you to live by my laws, and you will obey my rules. Then you will live in the land that I gave your ancestors. You will be my people, and I will be your God.

Ezekiel 36:26–28

After this, I will pour my Spirit on everyone.
Your sons and daughters will prophesy.
Your old men will dream dreams.
Your young men will see visions.
In those days I will pour my Spirit on servants,
on both men and women.

Joel 2:28–29

I baptize you with water so that you will change the way you think and act. But the one who comes after me is more powerful than I. I am not worthy to remove his sandals. He will baptize you with the Holy Spirit and fire.

Matthew 3:11

When you are put on trial in synagogues or in front of rulers and authorities, don't worry about how you will defend yourselves or what you will say. At that time the Holy Spirit will teach you what you must say.

Luke 12:11–12

I will ask the Father, and he will give you another helper who will be with you forever. That helper is the Spirit of Truth. The world cannot accept him, because it doesn't see or know him. You know him, because he lives with you and will be in you.

John 14:16–17

Peter answered them, "All of you must turn to God and change the way you think and act, and each of you must be baptized in the name of Jesus Christ so that your sins will be forgiven. Then you will receive the Holy Spirit as a gift. This promise belongs to you and to your children and to everyone who is far away. It belongs to everyone who worships the Lord our God."

Acts 2:38–39

Does the Spirit of the one who brought Jesus back to life live in you? Then the one who brought Christ back to life will also make your mortal bodies alive by his Spirit who lives in you.

Romans 8:11

At the same time the Spirit also helps us in our weakness, because we don't know how to pray for what we need. But the Spirit intercedes along with our groans that cannot be expressed in words. The one who searches our hearts knows what the Spirit has in mind. The Spirit intercedes for God's people the way God wants him to.

Romans 8:26–27

Now, we didn't receive the spirit that belongs to the world. Instead, we received the Spirit who comes from God so that we could know the things which God has freely given us.

1 Corinthians 2:12

Don't you know that your body is a temple that belongs to the Holy Spirit? The Holy Spirit, whom you received from God, lives in you. You don't belong to yourselves. You were bought for a price. So bring glory to God in the way you use your body.

1 Corinthians 6:19–20

You heard and believed the message of truth, the Good News that he has saved you. In him you were sealed with the Holy Spirit whom he promised. This Holy Spirit is the guarantee that we will receive our inheritance. We have this guarantee until we are set free to belong to him. God receives praise and glory for this.

Ephesians 1:13–14

Through him you, also, are being built in the Spirit together with others into a place where God lives.

Ephesians 2:22

Also take salvation as your helmet and the word of God as the sword that the Spirit supplies.

Ephesians 6:17

God revealed to the prophets that the things they had spoken were not for their own benefit but for yours. What the prophets had spoken, the Holy Spirit, who was sent from heaven, has now made known to you by those who spread the Good News among you. These are things that even the angels want to look into.

1 Peter 1:12

First, you must understand this: No prophecy in Scripture is a matter of one's own interpretation. No prophecy ever originated from humans. Instead, it was given by the Holy Spirit as humans spoke under God's direction.

2 Peter 1:20–21

Those who obey Christ's commandments live in God, and God lives in them. We know that he lives in us because he has given us the Spirit.

1 John 3:24

No one has ever seen God. If we love each other, God lives in us, and his love is perfected in us. We know that we live in him and he lives in us because he has given us his Spirit.

1 John 4:12–13

Redemption in Jesus Christ

He has sent salvation to his people.
He has ordered that his promise should continue
forever.
His name is holy and terrifying.

Psalm 111:9

O Israel, put your hope in the Lord,
because with the Lord there is mercy
and with him there is unlimited forgiveness.

Psalm 130:7

Because all people have sinned, they have fallen short of God's glory. They receive God's approval freely by an act of his kindness through the price Christ Jesus paid to set us free from sin.

Romans 3:23–24

Christ paid the price so that the blessing promised to Abraham would come to all the people of the world through Jesus Christ and we would receive the promised Spirit through faith.

Galatians 3:14

Through the blood of his Son, we are set free from our sins. God forgives our failures because of his overflowing kindness.

Ephesians 1:7

God has rescued us from the power of darkness and has brought us into the kingdom of his Son, whom he loves. His Son paid the price to free us, which means that our sins are forgiven.

Colossians 1:13–14

Realize that you weren't set free from the worthless life handed down to you from your ancestors by a payment of silver or gold which can be destroyed. Rather, the payment that freed you was the precious blood of Christ, the lamb with no defects or imperfections. He is the lamb who was known long ago before the world existed, but for your good he became publicly known in the last period of time. Through him you believe in God who brought Christ back to life and gave him glory. So your faith and confidence are in God.

1 Peter 1:18–21